THE BOUNCE BACK

Raw and uncut: My life. You thought you knew, but you have no idea.

By: Tiffani Rose

God Is My Bounce Back

Blessed in all things, good and bad, because God kept
me.

Optimistic in knowing hard times don't last always.

Understanding God's purpose for my life.

Nothing can stop me.

Calm that I had through many, many storms.

Everlasting love from God, no matter what I've done.

Beautiful in how God can change anyone, even me.

Asking God to come into my life again; but He never left
me.

Caring about how God thinks of me now.

King of Kings and Lord of Lords, now and forevermore in
my life.

Table of Contents

Chapter 1
The Greatest Man

Happiness is what I had as a child: great mother, wonderful stepfather, an "okay" older sister, and an in-and-out-of-trouble older brother. At a young age, I never knew that things would soon take a turn for the worse.

My stepfather, Leo Wherry, made rainy days sunny and dark days bright. Leo was great to my mother, Dixie Michelle Bell. She didn't allow us to call him Leo. "Papa" was what we called him. Papa was twenty-plus years older than my mother. It didn't matter to us. He was Papa! Papa had grown children, a daughter and son who lived in Wisconsin. We saw them when we traveled there.

Papa was great to us, giving us everything from great birthdays, wonderful Christmas mornings, vacations to Florida, California, Milwaukee, Chicago – you name it, he took us. He was a great provider. He's the only man I've ever known that loved to take us shopping at the mall and going downtown to get shoes. He was the greatest! He was my "dad," my superhero, my heart. I thought he was god!

Now, my brother Shawn on the other hand, didn't listen to Papa. He did what he wanted to do; not caring about the rules our stepfather laid out. Authority was something my brother didn't abide by. He sold drugs, hung with the wrong crowd, and never went to school. Shawn just loved being with his friends, the street gang YBI (Young Boys Incorporated).

Trouble was always around if it had something to do with my brother. Papa tried to be a father to him, but Shawn just wouldn't listen.

1980

Late one night my brother came running in the house. Blood was everywhere on him, dripping from his face and hands, as he was shot in the face with a .22 caliber gun. My mother and Papa were trying to keep him alert as my sister called the ambulance.

We rushed to the hospital, and the doctor saved my brother's life. But, the gunshot sent broken-off bullet fragments to Shawn's brain that they couldn't remove. The doctors told my mother and Papa that if he gets upset, he could drop dead. I was only four years old, but I remember all the blood and madness going on, and the story that I understood later in life, was the life my brother lived.

It was hell all around us as long as my brother Shawn was around. I'm now five years old and remember Mama and Papa going to the hospital because Shawn got stabbed in the arm and hand after a gang fight – this is during the time when the YBI and Pony Down gangs were really out of control. He survived so much and was so deep in the YBI gang, Papa couldn't talk any sense into him. If it wasn't one thing, it was another.

1982

I'm six years old; happy my brother is out of the house as I see my mother crying all the time, and it's because of my brother. Of course my mother loved my brother. She would still allow him to come around, even though Papa didn't agree.

One night, someone came and knocked at our door. We lived on a street where we were the only house on the block: 9641 Stopel off of Grand River in Detroit. So it wasn't a neighbor knocking, and friends or family would let us know before they just stopped by.

My mother looked out the window and opened the door. There were two guys asking about my brother and his whereabouts. I'm watching from the dining room as they questioned my mother. And to my shock and surprise, one of the guys pulled out a gun and said, "Bitch, you know where he is!" My mother stood there calmly and said, "I don't know. I really don't."

I heard a click. It was the guy trying to shoot the gun but it didn't go off. When he tried a second time, I was so scared, I stood there and wailed out a cry as I urinated on the floor. They saw and heard me, and ran off the porch.

My mother grabbed and held me and said, "It's okay. God was here." I didn't know what she meant then, but I do now. God was covering us and I didn't know it.

Papa was upset. He could have killed Shawn. As soon as Shawn popped back up, my father told him he couldn't come back there anymore. He cursed at

Papa, but that didn't faze him. He just wanted Shawn far away from there. It wasn't over with Shawn. There was always drama and violence surrounding him.

October 23, 1983

I remember this day so clearly because I turned seven years old. I had a party at a place called Major Magic's, an indoor playground for children. I was so excited because I got not only one, but two Cabbage Patch dolls. One was a baby named Melissa, and her big sister named Rebecca. I got a Barbie Dream House with five Barbie dolls, and a Barbie car. The only thing I didn't get was "Ken."

My mother and Papa didn't want me to have boy toys. It didn't matter, I was still happy. That was the best birthday ever!

The car ride home, I talked the whole time. I loved the dress I wore to my party, and didn't want to take it off. It was a cute Barbie dress, pink with little green flowers on it, and the Barbie stitching was in the corner at the bottom. My mother knew I loved it, that's the only reason she let me go to sleep in it.

Late into the night the whole house was sleeping, but we were awakened by a loud crash through our front window. We all got up, my mother, Papa, my sister San, and I. We all followed Papa very, very slowly through the dining room to the living room. I'm right on Papa's heels. And when he got close to the sofa, Papa pushed me away and told us all to go back – "go back," he said!

My mom, sister San, and I watched Papa as he moved the curtains off the sofa slowly, because whatever it was, it got tangled up and landed on the sofa. Papa yelled out, "It's a damn pipe bomb!" He dropped it back on the sofa and rushed us out the back door as he stayed in the house and called the police. I didn't know what a pipe bomb was, but I knew a bomb was bad.

Mama and Papa talked with the police as San and I sat in our car. Lights were flashing everywhere, and here comes a fire truck, an ambulance, and the most important vehicle that pulled up was the Bomb Squad.

Time was going by so slowly as officers from the Bomb Squad came in and out of our home. The whole street was on high alert as we sat far across the street watching. It was a success in dismantling the bomb!

See, here's another situation about God's greatness and how He'll cover you in times of trouble. The Bomb Squad told my mother and stepfather that the curtains and sofa stopped the bomb from going off. That if it had hit the floor, the whole house would have blown up.

I'm seven years old, not understanding why my mother walked around praising and thanking God for keeping us that night, but I truly understand now. Papa was so furious because he knew that bomb was meant for my brother Shawn. He just couldn't prove it. We did learn later that it was retaliation from the Pony Down gang to kill not only my brother Shawn, but his whole family. Papa made Shawn stay away. I don't know what he said to Shawn or how he did it, but Shawn stayed away this time.

CHAPTER 2
Life Without You

October 1984

Papa didn't go to church with us every Sunday. My mother didn't drive at the time, so Papa would drop us off. My mom would call Papa after a long day of services, and he would be right on time to pick us up. As a child, growing up in church meant that you were there from 8:30 a.m. to about 6:00 p.m. -- all day, like working a job.

After service was over, it's time for Mama to call Papa to pick us up. Mama called, and called, and called; no answer. She waited and called again, still, no answer. You saw the look on her face of concern, but she stayed calm. One of the members from the church took us home.

That particular Sunday was October 14, 1984, the day the Detroit Tigers won the World Series. It was a lot of activity on the streets. Out of all the madness, happiness, and excitement, our house was "pitch dark." Our dog Misty was on the porch whimpering and looking sad. My mom said, "What's wrong, Misty? Your papa didn't let you back in?"

Our church member stayed in the car to wait and see if things were okay. My mom opened the front door, cut on the living room lamp, and everything looked normal. My sister San and I walked slowly behind our mother as she tried to shield us from what I think my mom knew we were about to see. My mother called out his name; "Leo, I know you're here. The car is outside. Leo? Leo," she

11

said. Again, no answer.

As we turned the corner to the bedroom, we saw him laid across the bed. He was a tall, dark man, about 6'4", 220 pounds. He was dead!

You could tell that he was either taking off or putting on his clothes, as his pants were on, but you could see that he was holding his suspenders with one hand, and his chest with the other. His "wife beater" was soiled, as he may have choked and vomited while dying.

I'm seven-and-a-half years old, and I knew he was dead, but I still thought I could wake him up! "Wake up, Papa! Wake up!" "Mama, what's going on," I asked.

My sister is screaming at the top of her lungs. My mother just stood there numb with hurt and strength, all at the same time. It was so much commotion going on. I just wanted Papa to "wake up."

The ambulance has come, and by this time they said it was nothing they could do. Papa had been dead from the time he dropped us off at church. That had been hours ago. My mother blamed herself for not being there, saying she shouldn't have went to church all the time; she should have been there for her husband. That blame she had on herself was something that stuck with her for a long time.

It's October 20, 1984, the day of papa's funeral, and all I remember was he had on a gray suit in a silver casket. I cried the whole time. I missed my Papa. We wondered why a perfectly healthy man had a massive heart attack.

The singing made me cry even harder. And as they closed the casket, that's when I knew my Papa was gone.

October 23, 1984, a few days after burying Papa, it's my eighth birthday. I'm so sad that Papa is gone. I only remember getting a few Barbie dolls and some clothes. No party; just me, Mama, San, and a cake. My Papa was gone. The whole house was sad. My mother was so hurt because now her soulmate is gone.

Papa had been in my life ever since I was a year old. He wasn't my father by blood, but he was a father that always said I was his, and he never called us his stepchildren.

When he brought us around others, he always said, "These are my children." How was life going to be now? My mother tried to keep it together, but with only Papa's pension and social security, it wasn't enough. My mother made clothing for people on the side, but it still wasn't enough.

My brother Shawn popped back up. I guess now he can come around more since Papa was dead. He's selling drugs heavy now. Shawn gives my mother money and pays bills sometimes. But he was too far gone in the streets to know what was really going on in our home.

I remember my mother getting a call from Dittrich Furs downtown, and they asked to speak to a Dixie Michelle Bell or Leo Wherry; and she told them, "I'm sorry, I'm Leo's wife. He passed away a month ago." They told her she needed to come down and pick up a black Glama mink coat that Leo had bought her; paid in full. They told

13

her he was supposed to pick it up, but they hadn't heard from him. It was an early Christmas gift for her. My mother couldn't believe it. Papa was still loving my mother, even after death. That's the kind of man Papa was.

My brother took her downtown to pick up the coat, and she was on "cloud nine." They gave her a big long box with the mink inside. It was dark brown, but almost looked black, with her initials inside, "D.M.B." She was so happy. I remember my brother saying, "I wish I could have told Leo I loved him more, and to thank him for loving us." But it was too late.

As time went on, Mom was really trying hard to keep everything together. Things just weren't the same, and the money wasn't either. My brother was still trying to give my mother money, but after a while, she just didn't want any parts of his drug money. She told Shawn that, and he got mad, cussed at my mother and said, "Well, get on welfare, then."

My mother was on welfare before when San and Shawn were little, so it was nothing to her to get back on welfare again. See, when Papa was living, we had it good; no welfare or any kind of state assistance. But after Papa died, our lifestyle died with him. So, back to food stamps, Focus Hope boxes, Goodwill, and repeated clothing for me.

After a while, my mother lost our white house with the chipping paint, and lost the two cars we had. She couldn't afford it. She was just taking care of too much with two children. I'm an adolescent at the time, and my sister San is a teenager. We had to move. So, off to Burgess Street in Redford, Michigan we go!

Chapter 3
Sickness and Pain

Just before we moved out of our peeling white house at 9641 Stopel Street ... the place where we came home and found papa dead, the place where I saw someone try to kill my mother, the place my brother came to when he got shot in the face, and the place where a pipe bomb was thrown through our home and could have killed us, but it didn't go off; a place where there were happy memories as well, health issues attacked my mother.

One day my mother had a headache all of a sudden. I never heard her complain of ever having headaches, so this was truly something new. She complained, and complained that it was getting worse; and all in her same breath she went into a violent seizure.

My sister and her then-boyfriend Billy were trying to hold my mother still, as she was shaking all over, everywhere. I stood there and watched in horror in not knowing what was going on. We called 911, and the ambulance rushed her to the hospital. The doctors told us they were going to admit her and run some tests to see what was going on.

A few days have gone by, and the doctors had ran test after test after test. The doctors told us my mother had a brain tumor. While lying in her hospital bed, my mother said she felt fine and was ready to go home. They made her stay a few more days, as they were going over things to prepare her for surgery in removing the tumor.

15

A few days after being released, they scheduled her surgery. When she showed up for surgery, they ran more tests, and to everyone's surprise, the tumor was gone. The doctors didn't know where it went. All my mother said was, "It was nobody but God."

As soon as my mother got a chance to tell God's goodness, she did just that at church. Her testimony that Sunday had the whole church crying and praising God. All she kept saying was, "God healed my body," and the church went crazy with praise.

See, at nine years old, I saw miracles happen even during the painful times in our lives. But God truly kept us, and I didn't even know it. God will keep you in perfect peace, even in times of sorrow, pain, and sickness. I saw the pure strength that my mother had. I only saw her cry at Papa's funeral. But she still showed strength in her own sickness. She never showed herself being "weak."

Towards year-end 1985, my mother got another companion (I wouldn't say boyfriend). His name was Gene. It was short-lived though. I think my mother fell in love with him, but it just didn't work out.

Gene acted like he was going to get back with my mother, but I was caught in the middle. My mother would tell me, "Gene wants to see you. He bought you something." We would go over there, and she would stay outside. He would hug me and sit me on his lap and say, "Do you want me and your mother to get back together?" I would say, "Yes." He would give me a hug, give me money, and stick his tongue in my mouth. I knew it was wrong of him to do that because he would tell me, "Don't tell your mother or she would be mad at you."

I grew nervous and I didn't know what to do. This happened three more times, and finally I just told my mother I didn't want to go over there anymore. She asked why, and I still never told her what he would do; tongue-kissing me, fondling me, touching my chest, and telling me "don't tell." She never forced me to tell her why. She just stopped taking me over there. See, God was working on covering me even then.

Yes, he molested me. But what if I didn't tell my mother to stop taking me over there? Things could have gotten worse. They did, but not with that man.

My mother was a great mother to us. She was just physically sick, and may not have picked up on things that were going on in our lives because of that.

I don't blame God for anything. I don't really blame my mother. I never will. God has His way of using everything that has gone on in my life. Everything has a purpose according to His plan. I didn't know that then, but I truly know it now. God is the Keeper of my mind, body and soul.

1986

I'm now ten years old. I've never seen domestic violence until my sister San had gone through it herself. Months of dating her then-boyfriend, Billy, who caused her to not come home all the time; and when she did, she came home with a smart and sassy attitude toward our mother.

San is twenty years old. I'm guessing it's okay for her to stay out all night, but it wasn't okay for her to be sassy towards my mother, and to be mean and hateful toward me.

She had a cool boyfriend, so I thought. Billy and San were a cute couple. I never knew they were having problems, or should I say, he was giving her problems.

That summer of '86, I was told by my mother to go outside and get the paper. When I opened the front door, I couldn't believe my young eyes. Now, remember, I'm ten years old at this time. So what I'm looking at was truly not for my eyes. Pictures of my sister San's badly beaten, naked body were plastered all over our yard. I remember the poster board of the same brutal pictures on a wooden steak standing high for all the neighbors to see.

I ran and got my mother, crying, "Mama, San is in the yard. Pictures of San are in the yard." My mother came out and looked in disbelief. We both couldn't believe what we saw. San had been abused, and we didn't know at the time it came from Billy.

My sister San had broken up with him, and he was mad that she moved on with someone else. So Billy kidnapped my sister, choked her, beat and raped her, and took naked and bruised pictures of her to humiliate her even more.

My sister came home from somewhere, and my mother showed her what was in the yard. All she could do was cry. She couldn't believe it. San was scared of Billy. My mother wanted her to go to the police, but she didn't want to go. San was so embarrassed, that she and my mother kept that to themselves forever.

I loved my sister. At that time I wanted to be like her, but I don't think she ever loved me. She would jump on me and punch me in the stomach to where I couldn't breathe. She would pull my hair and just call me names for no reason.

I had a pretty good relationship with San while growing up until about ten years old. Things changed, and that's when San started to abuse me. It got so bad that I got tired of hiding it from our mother, and told her what San was doing. It got so bad that eventually my mother told her she had to move out. San got smart with my mother and said, "I'll move in with Raymond," her new boyfriend.

The abuse my sister gave me was of hurt and pain she was going through in her relationship with Billy. She didn't know how to love her little sister like a big sister should, so she did what she knew best. The abused had now turned into the abuser.

Shawn and San had the same father (Bobby Bell). I came along ten years later from a different father (Johnnie Jones). I never saw abuse before, but my brother and sister did from their father to our mother. Their father was married to my mother, and I heard stories growing up about how Bobby would beat the crap out of my mother for no reason. So I could just imagine what Shawn and San saw growing up, the abuse their father gave to our mother.

I have talked to God about the relationship with my sister, but as time moved on, so did I. For a long time, I would go back and forth with my feelings about whether or not I should reach out to her. It's probably best I just don't.

I have forgiven her now that I'm 40 years old. But like I said before, it's just best I don't deal with her. See, you can love your family, but if they do wrong by you, you really don't have to deal with them, and that's where I'm at today.

CHAPTER 4
Innocence Gone

1989

I'm thirteen years old. We've been living in our new neighborhood for about two years now. I love this neighborhood. I have new friends and going to a new school. We would walk to the corner store, play outside until the streetlights came on, and sneak around the corner to see our other friends. Every now and then the Swim Mobile would come into our neighborhood. (A Swim Mobile is a big truck with a pool, and the neighborhood kids would have a chance to swim and have fun.)

Life was really good at that time. We were poor, but happy. Some of my friends' parents worked. Some were collecting a welfare check like my mother, but it was nothing to any of us. We were all the same. My friends loved my mother because she would always give us a book of food stamps to get junk food.

My life would change that year. My mother was so sick from having seizures to where it got to a point that she would black out and hit her head all the time. Once she awoke, she would never remember what happened – just getting up a little groggy and moving on.

I think my mother's thoughts about her being sick was something she tried to just leave to God to take care of. And when other ailments would come her way, she would just say, "What's next?"

21

Summer 1989

There was a guy that would come over and do yard work, fix on things around the house, and after some time, my mother took a liking to him. I didn't like him from the start. He was nice to my mother, and tried to be nice to me. But even though I'm only thirteen years old, I felt he wasn't right.

Joseph Ambrose was his name; six feet, three inches tall, skinny, with patchy brown skin, and walked with a limp. He always went out of his way to be nice to me. He knew I didn't like him, so he worked hard to try to win me over by giving me a few dollars to go to the store with my friends -- just always trying to talk to me, trying to be nice.

Eventually, he moved in with us. I was so mad. At that time I'm thinking, "He doesn't have his own house? Why does he have to come here?" I could see my mother really liked him. A lot of times I would just go across the street to my friends, Teir or Tonya's house, just so I didn't have to see him.

One evening my mother had another bad seizure to where she fell in the bathroom and hit her head really hard. This time she wanted to go to the hospital. Other times before, she would want to just sleep it off. This time was bad.

Now we're at the hospital, and I'm praying they would just give her medicine or something and send her home. See, I felt this way because a few nights before, I was in our basement washing clothes, and Joe came up behind me and made me feel his penis. The look of enjoyment on his face made me vomit. He made me clean up my vomit and said, "If you say anything to your mother, I'll kill you and her."

That's all I kept thinking about as the doctors came and told us that my mother had to stay. I was so mad, that I knew I had to go home with him. My heart almost jumped out of my chest. The ride home was quiet. I looked across the street to see if my aunt and uncle were home, but they weren't.

As we pulled up to the house, I sat there for a few minutes as I was in a trance until he yelled at me to come on in the house. As we approached the front door, I felt like I'm going to come in here and he's going to make me kiss him or feel on him. Little did I know it was going to be much worse than that.

It was late when we came home from the hospital, so I changed into my pajamas and went to bed. I didn't fall asleep right away. I just laid there staring at the ceiling with my mind racing, as I was wondering what he was doing in the house. I had my door closed with a chair up to it, nervous and scared, just knowing something was going to happen.

I tried to fall asleep, but couldn't. I just laid there with a sick feeling of something not feeling right. And sure enough, I heard my chair move as he pushed open my bedroom door. There stood Joe, this six-foot-three-inch tall man with my mother's shotgun in his hand. He laid the shotgun on my bed and crawled up to me. His eyes were bloodshot red, even in the dark. I saw the sick look in his red eyes. I'm assuming he was drunk because I smelled alcohol on his stank breath.

He told me to take off my panties. I think he said it a few times because it made him rip my panties off in frustration that I didn't move fast enough.

I tried to get up and run, but he had all his weight on me. I felt him penetrate me. I fell sick with anger and madness at my mother for not being here to protect me. Mad because my Uncle Garland and Aunt Yvonne weren't home across the street. I was lost in hell, as it felt good to him and sickening to me.

I just stared at the ceiling with tears coming down my face. He then stopped, got up, and said, "I'm about to run you some bath water. Go take a bath and go back to bed."

I laid there for so long it seemed like hours. He came back in my room and I jumped, thinking he was coming to do it again. But he yelled at me and said, "Bitch, get up! I said take a bath. Don't make me do something to you." I didn't know he left the gun on the bed until he came back in there the second time. He saw the gun and grabbed it up and walked out the room.

I jumped up, went into the bathroom, and just sat in the tub. For whatever reason, I didn't wash up. I just sat there in a daze, not really knowing how my night was going to end.

He rushed me to come out of the tub so he could talk to me. He made me come in my mother's bedroom as he sat on the bed and I sat in a chair. He then started to apologize and said I made him do it. I asked, "Joe, are you serious? How did I make you rape me?" He said, "Bitch, you walk around mad at me because I'm here. You never tried to get to know me. I heard you talk about me to your mother and asking her, 'Why is he here? I hate him. I wish he would just leave.' That made me so mad, I just wanted to fuck that young pussy."

I started crying when he said that to me. I asked him, "Why are you here? You hate my mother and me so much. What, you just need a place to stay?" He said, "Shut up, bitch, shut up, shut up!" He was so drunk, he started tripping over himself. As he stumbled, he walked over to me and said, "I'm sorry, but you can't say anything. Please, don't. If you do, I'm going back to the penitentiary." I said, "What's the penitentiary?" He said, "Prison." I said, "You been to prison?"

I'm sitting there terrified. This man has been to prison, and for what? I never asked. I just watched him as he held my mother's shotgun in hand. I was just trying to figure out how to get out of there. Come on, Tiff, think. What can you do? If I made a run for it, he'll shoot me in the back. I grew numb all over again. Just the mere fact of him keeping me captive was so painful to me.

He rambled on and on, apologizing to me in a drunken state of mind, and telling me if I move, he'll kill me. He was drinking so heavily that I thought if he would just keep drinking, he would get drunk enough that he would pass out and I could get away.

It's the summertime. We didn't have air in the house, so it's burning up! I finally convinced him that I really needed to go outside and get some air. And after a little hesitation, he grabbed my mother's shotgun and we went outside on the porch.

We're sitting on the porch, and I'm thinking of how to get away. All the while, he's crying in a drunken cry, saying, "You're going to run away, aren't you?" I said, "No, I'm not. It's just hot in the house. I need some air."

He kept his hand on my neck, trying to keep a tight hold on me as we sat outside on the porch. I asked him again why he did that to me. "I'm not going to say anything, I just want to know why." He started crying again, saying, "You're going to tell. I know you are. I don't want to go back to the penitentiary."

I sat there praying that my Uncle Garland would pull up, as he was not home at the time.

My Uncle Garland married our neighbor across the street, a really nice lady named Yvonne. They were always hanging out as a couple. They were real night owls. I knew whenever they did come home, they wouldn't go to sleep. They always left the door open late into the night. So I'm just waiting for them to come driving up the street.

Joe is talking to me, pleading to me not to say anything. Growing tired, he was ready to go back in the house. But I knew if he took me back in the house, anything could happen. I just couldn't go back in.

It's about two-something in the morning. I knew this because he said, "It's 2:30. It's getting late. Let's go in." And sure enough, here comes Uncle Garland and Auntie Yvonne driving up the street. I was so happy, but I didn't let it show to Joe. Joe and I waved at them, and I really thought they were going to stop, but they kept going and pulled up in their driveway. We sat there for a few more minutes, and then Joe said, "Come on, let's go in the house."

I looked across the street and saw that my aunt and uncle left the front door open as always because they loved staying up late. As soon as Joe leaned over and picked up his drink off the porch, I made a dash for it! I ran so fast across the street. I was too scared to look back to see if Joe was going to shoot me with my mother's shotgun; but he didn't. It felt like I was running forever, because even though my aunt and uncle lived across the street, they lived diagonally. So the run seemed like forever.

I finally got on my uncle and aunt's porch. As I looked in, they were on their sofa watching television. They saw me, but I banged on the door anyway, yelling and screaming, "Joe raped me! Joe raped me!" My aunt jumped up and opened the screen door and grabbed me and said, "Tiffani, what did you say?" I said, "Auntie, Joe raped me. Mama is in the hospital." My uncle said, "For what? Is she sick again?" I said, "Yes. She had a seizure and hit her head on the bathtub, and they kept her. So I had to come home with Joe."

I'm crying hysterically. My aunt just held me as my Uncle Garland dashed across the street to my house to see if Joe was there. He ran over there so fast I didn't get a chance to tell him he had my mother's shotgun. But my uncle came back to his house where I was and said, "He's gone. He left."

My Aunt Yvonne had me take a shower. They didn't call the police, for whatever reason. Maybe they were trying to think of what to do next. That night my aunt showed me comfort and concern. She put me in one of her daughter's old bedrooms. Finally, I went to sleep.

Chapter 5
Dear Mama

The next day, my Uncle Garland and Aunt Yvonne took me down to the hospital where my mother was hospitalized; and there she was, a light-skinned, heavyset woman. Strong, but looking weak from being sick; she was so happy to see us. She told us to come in and sit down. She said, "I think they'll send me home in a few days, but I'm ready to go now."

My uncle and aunt didn't know where to start. My mother's name was Dixie. But she hated that name, so everyone called her by her middle name, Michelle. My uncle said, "Michelle, we have something to tell you." My mother had a confused look on her face, not knowing what my uncle was about to say to her. My mother said, "What's going on?" My Aunt Yvonne jumped in and said, "Joe raped Tiffani," as she knew my uncle couldn't get it out.

The look my mother had on her face was of hurt. But of pure curiosity she said calmly, "Okay." She asked my aunt and uncle to step out of the room. She wanted to talk to me. My mother asked me, "Tiffani, what happened?" As I told her, tears flowed down my face. I tried to tell her every detail, but she cut me off and said, "It's alright," with a hard, strong hug. She asked did we call the police. I told her no. They wanted to bring me to you first. I asked her, "Do you believe me?" She quickly said, "Yes!"

My mother leaned over and grabbed her nurse call button, and the nurse came in. She had me get my uncle

29

and aunt from the hallway to come back in the room. The nurse was told what happened to me, and they whisked me away to have tests done, and they called the police up there.

Everything was taken from me, including my panties and clothes. They had me open my legs and I began to cry. But, the nurses were so nice to me that they begin to make me comfortable doing so. I was so happy when it was over. I was ready to go home with my aunt and uncle. I didn't want to go back to my home. They told my mother I showed signs and evidence of being raped/penetrated.

A few days later my mother was back home. Two detectives came by and got as much information and evidence from our home needed to apprehend Joseph Ambrose. They confiscated my mother's shotgun, and they already had the clothing that I had on for evidence. And from that point on, they were on it until they caught Joseph Ambrose a few days later.

My mother talked with me, prayed for me, and loved on me. I was actually shocked that she did that, not that she didn't love me or never believed me. I just remember a few friends that had been molested and raped, and their mothers blamed them; called them whores and told them, "You wanted him and you're lying."

For some crazy reason, I thought that's how my mother was going to be towards me. Wow, my mom, she was so loving and supportive. So supportive that I didn't even have to go to court. She spoke on my behalf in court, and fought for me. Joe Ambrose received a sentence of seven to fifteen years in prison for what he did to me.

My mother came home and told me the great news! I was so happy that Joe and all his threats, apologies, and limp-walking self was locked away for a long time.

My mother sat me down on the sofa with a loving, concerned look on her face and said, "Tiffani, I love you, and I never want to hurt you, nor do I want anyone else to hurt you. So in saying that, as long as I live, I will never, ever bring another man around you or in our home. I promise, from now on, it's just me and you, and I need you to feel protected and safe."

All of this was hard on my mother. My mother was a great mother. Things that happened to me could have been avoided if she wasn't so sick, and a lot of times incoherent. But I'm glad she showed me that even through her weakness she was strong enough to stand up for me.

See, God still covered me in this time of my life. The violations that were done to me, not once, but twice, by grown men who knew better not to do something sexual to a child, was something I couldn't understand.

Truly knowing God now shows me that He was covering me, because Joseph Ambrose could have killed me. The devil could have attacked my mother's mind causing her to believe Joe, thinking otherwise. But none of that happened. God kept me through all that madness and pain, keeping my mind; not having a nervous breakdown later in life, and now allowing me to see just how much God was covering me. I didn't know it then like I know now.

Thank you, God, for saving me!

Chapter 6
Real Sisters

Late 1989

This lady named Lisa Browning who lived next door to us was always so nice to my mother and I. She was a "Corporate America" working lady, married with no children. She was "fly;" hair was fly, drove a fly car. And when I look back at where we lived, she surely didn't seem like she would live in that neighborhood.

In 1988, when she moved next door to us, she would speak and I would run over there because I wanted to see the kind of shoes she had on and the suits she would wear. I looked up to her, wishing she would just let me come over and just talk. Eventually, she did.

Lisa was and still is nice and sweet. She knew my mother was sick. She knew we used to go to church every Sunday, but my mother was too sick to go anymore. So, Lisa asked my mother if she could start taking me to church, taking me under her wings ... my wishes came true.

She turned out to be my big sister; the sister I wished San could have been, but wasn't. She catered to me and listened to me about things I couldn't tell my mother. A ray of hope that made me believe I could grow up and be just like her.

Lisa was hurt when I told her that Joe raped me. Our sister relationship had grown to a point that she made me feel like family, and her family made me feel like family as well. Lisa took me everywhere. To this day, I feel like I truly belong to a "real" family.

1990

Lisa was moving. She was getting a divorce from her husband, and she moved on. I was devastated. I no longer had my sister next door to me. But, Lisa never stayed away from me. Lisa came and got me every weekend, and when she had to take me back home, I was back to my reality at 9606 Decatur Street.

Lisa was the best thing that ever happened to me. Lisa is one beautiful lady, inside and out. She's five feet, six inches tall; blonde, short hair; back then about 140 pounds. She wore contacts back then, and was and still is one of the most stylish women I know. She always showed concern of how I was doing in school, but I never told her I was skipping school and running around. I thought she wouldn't want me around anymore if I told her that.

Lisa was/is my sister. I remember times when my blood sister San would see Lisa and roll her eyes at her. I talked about Lisa so much when San came around. She would get mad and would even say, "Fuck that Bitch! I don't want to hear about what you did with her this weekend."

The pure hate that San showed towards Lisa when she saw her was the same way San felt about me, and I was her blood. Lisa never paid San any mind. Her concern and love was always put towards me. It's amazing how someone could not be your blood relative and love you unconditionally, and their family too.

Lisa would take me shopping. We'd go to the movies. She talked with me, and truly taught me how to love. That's all I ever wanted in a big sister. And again, she did just that and still does today. She's 52 years old now, and I'm 40. She's been in my life ever since I was 11-1/2 years old, and no one can ever take her place; not anyone.

See, God knew what I needed at that point in time of my life. My mother was there, but she was too sick to really be a mother, do things with me, and really try to mold and shape me into what I needed to grow up to be.

My mother would lay in the bed and talk with me and try to give me advice. But the best thing she ever did was allowing Lisa to come into my life. My mother wasn't jealous of the relationship Lisa and I had. God was blessing me with certain people in my life. I didn't know it then like I know now.

Chapter 7
Young and Dumb

Summer 1993

I'm 16 years old. I'm outside on a hot 80-degree day. My friend-turned-cousin after my uncle and her mother got married, Teir, and I were just laughing and playing around. Our friend Tonya came out and joined us as we walked to the store, came back, and did a whole lot of nothing.

Later that day I see a funny color blue Honda Accord with blue and white piped-out seats (as they called it back then), which were seats one color and trimmed with another color around the edges. Inside the Honda Accord driving was a guy I had never seen before. I looked over and asked my cousin Teir, "Do you know who that is?" Have you ever seen him before?" She said, "I don't know his name, but I've seen him over in the neighborhood driving around. I think he knows the guy O who lives around the corner. I've seen O in the car with him before." I said, "Hmm," as I'm thinking about how I could meet him.

Days went by, and the guy in the blue Honda didn't cross my mind.

I go to the store with one of my friends, K. We never walked straight to the store and back. We always did a little detour to see our friends around the corner on Carlin Street. And to my surprise, here comes the guy in the blue piped-out Honda Accord. He pulled up at O's house. I

35

found out who O was because my friend K started dating O's nephew.

We stopped at O's house as well, and that was my opportunity to get the guy in the blue Honda to notice me. He's talking to O while sitting in the car as K and I stand in front of the house waiting on O's nephew. I asked K, "Who is that?" She said, "Girl, that's Tron." I'm like, "Tron? That's a funny name." But I didn't care about that. I was attracted to the five-foot, ten-inch, dark-skinned man with white teeth. He weighed about 230 pounds, wore a long gold chain, gold watch, jeans and a black t-shirt.

I had a thing for a rough-looking but clean guy, and I also had a thing for a guy in the streets. That's all that I lived around. Just about all the neighborhood guys were selling drugs. A few were my short-lived boyfriends. I left them behind and moved on because I wanted something with this guy Tron.

As O got out of the passenger seat of Tron's car and began to close the door, Tron said, "Hey, Baby Girl, come here." I didn't know any better. I didn't know that a real man is supposed to approach, not tell you "come here," and I walk up to a car. I didn't care. I got his attention. At that time, I'm five-feet six inches tall, slim but with a thick build, about 130 pounds, small chest, little waist, and a big, huge butt! I'm assuming that's what got his attention.

As I walked close to him, he told me, "I love you, hazel eyes." I started to smile as I grabbed the end of the ponytail I had in my hair, trying to act bashful. He never asked how old I was until later. I gave him my number, and he gave me his beeper number and told me to call him anytime; and so I did.

The next day he came on my block driving slowly with O in the car, looking for me. I was outside, so I didn't hear the house phone ring. I was so excited he came looking for me. So he asked, "Can you go somewhere with me?" I said, "Where?" He said, "Flint."

I didn't know where or what Flint was. He said, "It's about an hour away," as he saw the confused look on my face. I said, "How long will we be gone?" He said, "You'll be back about 10:00 p.m." I said, "Okay," as I knew I was going to lie to my mother about being either over Teir's or Tonya's house. I had it all planned out. I was going somewhere with Tron.

That night we're in Flint. I was around Tron and so many other guys that I knew from the neighborhood, so I felt safe. But time was flying by, and 7:00 p.m. came, 8:00 p.m. came, 9:00 p.m. came, 10:00 p.m. came, and 11:00 p.m. came and gone. I'm still in Flint. I didn't say anything to Tron, as I didn't want to look like a kid. So I just sat with him and the other guys and waited on Tron to finish what he was doing -- cooking dope, counting money, smoking weed, and drinking. It was a "trap house" we were in, and everything they were doing went well into the night.

It's about 3:00 a.m., and everyone was leaving but Tron and I. He said, "Baby, I'm too tired to drive back down to Detroit, but I'll take you home first thing in the morning." With an uncertain stare, I said, "Okay." That's the first time I stayed out all night. Never had I done that before. All I could think about was what in the world my mother was going to say and do to me? My mother had a seizure the day before. I knew she would be groggy and weak, so I took advantage of that and stayed out with Tron. Her feeling that way wouldn't last long, so I had to hurry up and get home.

It's twelve noon, I was supposed to be home by 10:00 p.m. the night before. As we pulled up on the street, everyone seemed to be outside waiting, talking, and wondering where I was. I told Tron to stop at the corner, as I saw my mother standing outside in her housecoat, looking furious. Tron gave me about seven hundred dollars, and I gave him a kiss, got out the car, and walked down the street to my house. As I approached my mother and the other neighbors standing there, all my mother said was, "See y'all later."

"Come on, Tiff!" Very calmly my mother told me to sit down on the sofa, and quickly said, "Tiffani, I saw that guy when he drove past. How old is he?" I said, "I don't know!" She said, "I know he's twenty-four." I looked in shock and said, "How do you know?" She said, "The neighbors told me. Now, Tiff, I don't want you around him. He's too old for you." But I didn't listen. I said to her, "Okay, Mama," just so she could stop talking. She didn't put me on punishment or hit me. She just walked away and I went my way.

I didn't sleep with Tron that first night, but there were many nights after that. We were together so much I never knew he had a woman and other children. I stayed out all night with him most nights. And every time we were together, we had sex. Any chance Tron and I got, we slept together, and I always came home with money.

My mother was pissed. She just stopped telling me he was no good for me. My mother giving me the silent treatment hurt me worse than her whipping me. When she finally talked to me, she said, "Tiff, if you keep on with this kind of behavior, you're going to end up pregnant." Sure enough, October of 1993, I got pregnant right after my birthday, and I didn't even know it.

Chapter 8
Growing Pains

It's February 1994. I'm seventeen years old, and I'm going about my little life, still going to school, but skipping. Still messing around with Tron, but not as much. I came home from school, and I'm bending over to pick something up, and my mother walked in and said, "Tiff, are you pregnant?" I was shocked and looking stupid all at the same time. I said, "I don't know." She said, "You're pregnant, Tiff. I can tell."

That next week I went to the doctor, and, yes, they told me I was pregnant; about eighteen weeks to be exact. I was devastated. I called Tron and told him, and we decided I was going to get an abortion before I turned twenty-four weeks. I didn't tell my mother about it. What she told me was, "I'm going to be there for you, and try to help you with this baby." Little did she know I was planning to get an abortion.

The next day I'm on the phone with the abortion clinic, and my mother overheard me. She slammed the phone down and said, "Didn't I tell you we're going to be okay? I'm going to help you take care of this baby, and you're going to finish school. I don't care how sick I am. I'm going to help you. Now, that's it."

I felt a sense of disappointment because we were already poor. I had no job, no money, and a fly-by-night, so-called boyfriend. But most of all, my mother was sick and telling me everything was going to be fine, and I'm wondering how.

My belly is growing every day, and my mother is planning a baby shower. I wasn't happy. I'm really disgusted with myself. I felt like a disappointment to not just my mother, but everyone else. I received a lot of gifts, well wishes, and more. But when it was all over, reality set in that a baby was on the way.

July 26, 1994

My mother and I go to the doctor. I'm a week past my due date, and the doctor wants to check me out. I'm so nervous. I didn't know what was going on, really. As he checked me out, he told us that he's keeping me to induce my labor. I'm really nervous now. My mother was calm and was keeping me calm by praying for the baby and I.

The process was slow but fast. Early that next morning my mother was sitting there by my bedside talking to me, and all of a sudden she started to have a seizure. I couldn't believe it. My heart sank. And as they whisked her off to admit her, I was going into labor. My sister San finally made it. Someone I didn't want there, but at that moment she was helpful and supportive.

That day on July 27, 1994, at 11:08 a.m., I gave birth to a six-pound, ten-ounce baby girl. I already had her name picked out; "Tiana Michelle Bell."

I was only in the hospital two days, but before I left, I went down to see my mother. She really wasn't doing well. She wanted to see her granddaughter, but couldn't. She asked me if I stuck to the name. I said I had. I said, "Yes, Mama. I named her after you, using your middle name; Tiana Michelle Bell." My mother was so ready to go. She

41

grew frustrated, but she really needed to stay this time. Her seizures were getting worse.

Now it's time for me and the baby to go home. My mother is still in the hospital for a few more days. My sister San came to the hospital to pick Tiana and I up and take us home. I had no help from her. She just said, "Okay, you're on your own," walked out of the house and pulled off.

I just wanted my mother. I only knew how to feed Tiana and how to change her by the nurses at the hospital. I was really struggling with Tiana, but I soon got the hang of it. I would hold her all day and night until she fell asleep. I just asked God to help me with this baby until my mother came home four days later.

Finally, my mother is home. I am so happy to see her. She's so weak now, and it's from cancer.

Back in 1992, my mother had breast cancer. She had her left breast removed, and had undergone chemotherapy and radiation. Now, in January of 1994, months before Tiana is born, she got breast cancer again in the right breast. She never told anyone but San and I. She had radiation treatments to kill the cancer, but after months of radiation, it had spread; and she's still having seizures too.

My mother was truly not doing well. She could have gotten the other breast removed, but she said she just didn't want to be cut on anymore.

My mother was sick with so many health issues, until I didn't perform well in school. My mind was at home with her, and now I have a baby. I really couldn't go. My mother always tried to stay strong and help out with Tiana, but it was starting to be too much. I said to myself, "I knew I should have had an abortion."

August has come and gone. No Tron around to see Tiana. He's telling people the baby is not his. I felt mad, hurt, and ashamed that I loved this man so much. And now that Tiana is here, you throw us away like garbage. The neighborhood is telling him, "That's your baby. You need to do what's right." But he didn't come back around.

September has come and gone. Here comes October. It's my birthday month. I'm getting ready to turn eighteen, but I'm still just barely going to school, and trying to have a life with friends. I took advantage of my mother being weak and sick, but still alert, by leaving Tiana with her a lot. I wasn't ready to be a mother. I felt like I could still do what I wanted to do; my mother is here with the baby.

November 14, 1994

My mother had another violent seizure this time. But because my mother hated hospitals, she did like she's done in the past and said she wasn't going to the hospital. The seizure was so violent, I couldn't hold her still, and she fell over and bumped her head badly. The cancer was taking over and the seizures would not stop.

The look she gave me the next day when I was going to call 911 was "you better not call. I'm not going through this again." She said, "I'm tired of them poking me, telling me I need surgery, I need chemo, I need this, I need

that, maybe we need to change your medicines again."
She was tired, but I didn't know *that* tired.

November 18, 1994

I went to school, but before I left I asked my mother,
"Do you want me to stay home?" She said, "No."

Tiana was such a good baby. She slept all day with
very little troubles. She was only four months old, so it was
really nothing to feed her, change her, and put her back in
her bassinette.

My mother said, "Yes, Baby, go to school," in a
sweet, loving, calm, peaceful voice. I went to school, but
left early because I had a feeling something wasn't right. I
get home, and my mother was still in a peaceful space.
She was talkative, but soft and sweet. Not really energetic,
but alert.

She told me she fed Tiana, sang to her, and prayed
over her. I said, "Prayed? Why did you pray? Is
something wrong?" She said, "No, Baby. I just prayed for
peace." I was so puzzled as to why she said she prayed
for peace over a baby. But, hey, I'm young. My mother
was always praying. So I just figured that was her way of
relaxing and keeping her mind off her illnesses.

As the day went on, going into the evening, I walked
into my mother's room to tell her I'm going to take a quick
nap before I go to my friend Tia's house to get my hair
done. She said, "That's fine, Baby. I'll watch Tiana again
for you."

I must have overslept because Tia called to say, "Are you still coming to get your hair done?" I said, "Oh, my goodness! I'm on my way!"

As I jumped up to run in my mother's room, I said, "Ma, I'm late. I'm getting ready to go!" She didn't answer. I said, "Ma, Ma, Ma." I cut on her light, and my mother was a faint pale blue. I said, "Ma." I shook her, slapped her, and yelled at her; still, no answer.

I grabbed the phone, called my sister San, and said, "Mama's not breathing. Can you come over here," in a panicked voice. She said in a smart-mouthed tone, "Call the ambulance." I called 911, and they came in about five minutes. They worked on her and worked on her. A fire truck pulled up, and my Uncle Garland came running across the street, yelling, hollering, and screaming, "What's going on!"

They finally put my mother in the back of the ambulance and worked on her some more. San and her husband pulled up and rode to the hospital with my mother. I stayed behind. About two to three hours went by, and then my sister San pulled up. I ran outside and said, "She's okay. She'll be home in a few days." San said, "She's gone, Tiff." I said, "She's gone?" She said, "Yes, she's dead."

I screamed so hard and loud, my heart just sank. I cried so much that it made Tiana cry, as she's a baby and has no clue of what's going on. San tried to hug me and say it's okay, but it didn't feel loving and sincere. As people came over that night, I just wanted them to leave.

45

The hardest part of that night, November 18, 1994, was when my sister didn't ask me to come home with her so we could mourn together. She began, along with her husband, taking furs out the house that my stepfather bought my mother. Taking the only TV we had, along with other personal things of my mother's: the little cash my mother had, clothing, and other items. I couldn't believe what I was seeing. She looked at me as, "Mama's gone now; I don't have to be bothered with you anymore."

I was pissed that our mother wasn't dead five hours, and she's already taking things out the house. We argued, and one of my cousins stopped us and told her to leave. I told everyone I needed some private time, and made everyone leave. I was distraught about everything going on. I felt like I couldn't breathe.

The next day, friends came over trying to comfort me and be there for me. My uncle was so hurt and upset that his baby sister had died, he couldn't get his mind right to be there for me, but he was later. It was so hard for him until he began to question God. It was hard on us all!

I was hurt, but for some strange reason I was at peace that God called my mother home. No more cancer, no more seizures, no more meds, no more bills that she couldn't pay, and no more all-around suffering. Her soul was at peace.

The funeral was planned without me. My mother didn't look like how I remembered her to look. Sickness had taken its toll on her, but that was still my beautiful mother. She wore a black dress with pearls. She was a light-skinned woman, but meds and sickness made her skin darker. Through it all, she was still my mommy.

She laid in what we called a welfare casket -- a cheap casket that usually poor folks would get when they couldn't afford the metal caskets. I didn't realize it wasn't a good casket until the funeral directors went to close it and it wouldn't close. My mother's body was too big for it. That left a horrible memory in my mind.

I felt like my sister could have done better in burying our mother, and definitely in her final resting place. My sister had her laid to rest in a grave where I heard they stack people on top of one another way in the back. My mother doesn't have a headstone. We were poor, so I guess that's what you get with the little to no funds we had.

My sister San was just "dirty" towards my mother, and so it was no big surprise about how she had our mother buried. My sister didn't shed a tear one time; not at the house, not at the funeral, not afterwards. If she did, it was fake. She hollered out at the funeral, but no crying. I could have smacked her!

I stayed away from San the whole day of the funeral, the repass, and the cemetery. I just wanted no parts of her negative energy. I was so ready for Tiana and myself to just go home.

The day was over. I walked in the house away from all of the people who came in and out during this time. I could still smell my mother's sweet scent. After I changed and fed Tiana, I laid her down and she went to sleep. I walked in my mother's room, and the same sheets were on the bed since the day she died.

I was filled with so much emotion. I crawled in her bed, hugged her pillow, and cried. Her raggedy Bible was still laying there, and all I could say to the Bible was, "Why right now, God?" I felt relieved she was gone, but had a selfish way of wanting her here. "I love you, Mama. I love you!" I said that so much and cried so much that I cried myself to sleep.

The pain was there for a long time. Caring for Tiana was starting to be a piece of cake. It would get hard from time to time, but we saw it through. Getting on welfare was my next step until I could figure out how I was going to find a job. It's not just me; it's the both of us, Tiana and I.

Thanksgiving, Christmas, and the New Year had come and gone. I was not going to school. I tried, but I didn't have a babysitter to watch Tiana.

My sister Lisa stepped in and took me back to Mackenzie High School; I soon after dropped out. Four years later, I received my GED.

Chapter 9
A New Start

March 1995

I received a call that my great-grandmother passed away (Babe "Rose" Robinson). My namesake lived 100 years, and now has gone home to be with God.

My great-grandma was sweet, stern, loving, and kind. She didn't have a lot, but she made us feel loved. I can remember us going to her house in Mount Clemens, Michigan, waking up at 6:00 a.m., ready to eat biscuits made from scratch. My great-grandma would start at 4:00 a.m. We ate biscuits with jam preserves while sitting around watching her crochet blankets and sweaters -- just remembering the good times.

I loved going to Mount Clemens, especially when my cousin Channon would come to town from Denver, Colorado, my Uncle Garland's son. We would have so much fun seeing all my cousins, aunts, and uncles. We had happy times. But after Big Mama Babe passed, that all faded away.

Now it's time for the funeral. I got to see some of my family again. It has been five months after my mother's death, and family keeps asking me how Tiana and I are doing. I always replied and said, "We're doing just fine."

I saw my sister San, and we didn't speak. I couldn't believe what I saw her in. It was the mink coat our stepfather bought our mother right before he died. I just laughed at her, as it wasn't even that cold outside. So, she really looked like a fool. She was so desperate to wear her dead mother's mink coat; she looked crazy!

Some of the family knew San and I weren't talking, but I didn't care. I just wanted to see Mama Babe one last time and go home.

It's April 1995. I heard a hard banging knock at the door. I go to the door and it's a bailiff serving foreclosure papers. I asked, "What is this?" I didn't know what foreclosure was. I'm eighteen years old, and never paid a real bill before. He said, "You have just a few days to try and redeem the house back." I later found out the mortgage hadn't been paid in months, and the taxes in years.

When I did talk to my sister she told me that she was paying the mortgage for my mother while she was alive and after. But that wasn't true. She had not paid it right before our mother died or after. When my Uncle Garland did his research, he was so upset with my sister. He had already paid a $600 water bill and other bills at our house, and gave money for Tiana and I. But when he tried to see how much it would be to redeem my mother's house, it was just too much to get it back. My hatred for San grew EVEN STRONGER!

I called my "sister" Lisa, and told her what was going on. Lisa didn't ask any questions. She got her nephew Terrence, fiance' Mike and others to help move myself, Tiana, and the raggedy old furniture I had from my mother out of the house. I was so happy that my life over at 9606 Decatur was about to be a thing of the past.

Lisa and Lisa's niece Dawn (but we call her Doni) would take turns helping me with Tiana as much as they could. After a while, I guess you could say I got comfortable at Lisa's to where I thought I could do what I wanted to do. I would stay out late, go places and not say where I was going and when I was coming back to the point where Lisa was getting frustrated with me and wanted me to move out.

She discussed with her niece Doni about me coming over there. I just didn't know it. So one day I knew it was getting close for Lisa to try to find somewhere else for me to live, and I faked like I took a whole bottle of pills, but I didn't. I thought Lisa would have sympathy for me, acting like I was going to kill myself, and let me stay.

I was doing so much that wasn't to Lisa's liking, and she was nothing but good to Tiana and I. I didn't appreciate her and all she had done. So it was time for Lisa to let me go, or so I thought.

See, Lisa never wanted me out of her life. She just thought it would be a better fit if I lived with her niece Doni. Doni was seven years older than me. I'm eighteen; she's twenty-five. Doni is our modern day Pocahontas; light skin with dark features, black hair, full-figure, feminine build, stern, but loving. That's what I needed – stern, but loving.

Lisa was somewhat passive, but not a pushover. Lisa was sweet, but not aggressive enough to deal with my intolerable behavior.

Doni, on the other hand, had taken care of adults that were older than her. So, me coming over to Doni's house was nothing for her. I was a piece of cake.

11111 Courville, Detroit, Michigan; I'm on the east side now. This is new to me. I knew nothing but the west side of town, so I had some learning to do. It was cool; Doni made Tiana and I feel right at home.

We would sit on the flowered sectional Doni had and talk while she cooked. We cleaned. Doni would do my hair for me, as she was a licensed cosmetologist. She left Charlene's Hair Salon and started doing hair from home. She made way more money doing so.

I saw Doni's work ethic, but I didn't grasp onto it. One day she said, "Tiffani, what are you going to do? You've got this baby here. You need a job." I told Doni, "I don't need a job. I got my welfare check." She had steam coming out of her head. She said, with a beet-red face, "You gone get the fuck out of here if you don't get a job!" She couldn't believe I said that. As I look back, I can't believe I said it either.

I was truly not supposed to be a mother. I hadn't taken Tiana to the doctor for more shots. I didn't want to get on the bus to find a job. I truly thought my poor ass was too good for the bus and working a minimum wage job.

One day I came home from going to the beauty supply for Doni, and sitting in the living room was one of Doni's friends who was an officer of the court named LaLette. She told me if I don't get it together with Tiana, her immunization shots, and me working, she can have

Tiana taken away from me. Ms. LaLette talked with me for so long that day that it truly had my mind racing.

I ended up allowing Doni to take Tiana for about three months, as Doni always made it clear that if I didn't want her, she'll take her. My friends bashed me and told me Tiana was mine. "Go get your baby. Doni just wants your welfare check." It was just too much going on. I had Doni in one ear, and friends in the other.

I was scared of Doni. She always threatened to jump on me, and I knew she would. But that was because she would be so mad at how I was acting and how I was as a mother. There were times when it could have been a stomp-down, drag-out fight with Doni and I about Tiana. Then would come Ms. LaLette, our mediator, the one who could talk sense into both of us.

Time went on and it got better between Doni and I. She loved Tiana and I, and she always wanted what was best for us. All the arguments, "threats," and cursing me out was her way of putting in hard work for the ones she loved. I truly appreciate her for that.

It's much more to the relationship with Lisa (my sister) and Doni (my niece that's older than me) by way of "adoption," not blood-related.

I didn't write every up and down, in and out, good and bad time in this book. I've been in their lives ever since I was 11-1/2 years old. Now I'm forty, and they know we've been through a lot. They've loved me, been there for me, prayed for me, and stepped up when blood relatives were nowhere around. The love Doni and Lisa gave Tiana and I was, and still is, pure and unconditional. They tried to mold me, shape me, and make me a better woman.

I made the choice to grow up and be the way I was at one point in time in my life. But out of all the madness, the two of them never, ever, not once, gave up on me! Prayer changes things, or so they thought.

Chapter 10
Love Under New Management

Summer 1996

I'm working in a clothing store, Contempo, and got in trouble for what we call "hooking my friends up." My friend Bianca got in trouble as well, being on the receiving end. Bianca moved on with her life. She went to college, and now working in the auto industry.

I stayed in retail. I got fired, of course, from Contempo. I was cool with a manager named Kesha at a shoe store called Wild Pair. I used to hook her up when I worked at Contempo. So when she found out I had been fired, she offered me a job. That led me from Eastland Mall in Harper Woods, Michigan, to Fairlane Mall in Dearborn, Michigan to be an assistant manager there. I was excited!

Not only was I an assistant manager, I had a second job at a hip fashion forward store called Dolce Vita. I had two jobs, and I was buying my daughter and myself anything I wanted.

I'm working in a shoe store that sold regular shoes, boots, exotic dance shoes, and accessories. Sales were always good. I worked by myself a lot in the store. And with that came my little criminal mind wondering.

I saw the store manager one day return something for another employee that wasn't there, and they later came and picked up their money. And when I saw that, my mind started racing. I picked up on falsifying refunds. I would take shoes from the back that were worn and had been returned, and ring them up like someone walked in with them to return them. But it was all me! I got away with it for a long, long time. I'm taking money, shopping In Saks buying Via Spiga, Ferragamo -- anything I wanted, I got it.

I thought at nineteen I was doing something, until I came to work. The store manager, Chris, and Corporate were there with all the paperwork laid out with what I was doing. They asked why I did it, and other questions. In the end, they just fired me and took my keys.

I'm nineteen and I lost my main job. I'm on my way to my second job, Dolce Vita. My second job didn't pay a lot, but it was a job. I went to other stores trying to apply, but nothing came through.

While at Dolce Vita, I'm working in the evening with two other girls, and a rough-looking guy came in with another guy clean-cut, and a young lady. I knew they were not from here (Detroit) because their accents were different and heavy. They just stood back and talked while the young lady shopped with me. When the young lady was done, one of the guys spent about $1,800 in the store that evening. I didn't think anything of it. I was just happy to get the sale.

Later that evening one of the guys called into the store and said, "Is the lady with the short blonde hair there?" I said, "This is she." He said, "I just left out the store with the guy and the lady. I was wondering if you have a man." I said, "No," real quickly. I saw the money he spent on her, and I was stuck on that. I'm nineteen, lost my job, wondering how I was going to make up for the money I lost. So I just wanted to see what he had to offer.

His name was Paul from Philadelphia, Pennsylvania. He was a rough-looking, sweet, and compassionate man.

He left two days after he called me at the store, but saw me before he left. Tiana was with the sitter. I didn't have a car yet to meet him, so I had him come over to my apartment.

He came with two other guys. Why I wasn't nervous, I don't know. But even though they looked rough, I felt at ease. He walked in, looked around, and saw I didn't have any furniture except a cheap dining set and nothing to sleep on in my one-bedroom apartment. He said, "Baby Girl, what you need?" I said, "Huh?" He said, "You need EVERYTHING! Nothing is in here."

He told me, "I don't know how much furniture costs here in Detroit, but when I get home, I will wire you some money. In the meantime, here's $3,000. Go out and find you some nice furniture. If you find something that costs a little more, I'll send more. I'm coming back in a week. I'll help you."

I said, "Why you want to help me so bad? You don't even know me." All he said was, "I like you." Paul and the other two guys picked up and left. Wow, that was strange!

I stood in my empty living room and thought I was in a dream. I just met him. There wasn't any time to get to know him. I didn't sleep with him, but I knew eventually I would have to. No man is just going to give you money like that and not expect something in return.

A few days passed, I called him; no answer. He called the next day and stuck to his word. He would wire money every few days. And when I was going to Western Union too much, he would have people from here bring me money.

Two weeks went by, and Paul had given me about $10,000. I had only seen him twice; once in the store, and the one time he came to my apartment. Paul drove in from Philly after he left New York. He was always back and forth between New York and Philly. But once he was done, he came to Detroit.

It's about 3:00 a.m., and I'm excited he's here! He said I made him happy that I did right by the money he gave me. I didn't just take the money and buy clothes and shoes. He walked into my apartment filled with furniture and a place to lay his head when he came into town. I didn't have a car yet, but he made that happen by buying me a 1996 Mazda 626, green with cream interior. I was on top of the world!

The next night I felt it was time to give this man something. Oh, I took the money he gave me and bought him something -- a few clothes and Timberlands. Timberlands were his thing. He was from Philly. That's what they wore.

Now, I wanting Paul in the worse way, but he never rushed me into having sex with him. Paul had to be about twenty-six years old. I really don't know. All I know is that he was good to my daughter and I.

Later that evening after the whole car excitement died down, I finally let him meet Tiana. I never wanted men around my daughter because of what happened to me at a young age. I never told him my past, but he understood my thought process. He was so happy to see the child he was taking care of in the background. We went to dinner and later dropped her off to the sitter. We came back to the apartment and slowly made love. Nothing was rushed. He took his time with me. Paul was passionate, loving, and attentive to all my needs.

We talked, and he asked me if I liked Detroit. I told him, "Yeah, it's cool. Why?" He said, "I just asked. I do want you to come to Philly sometimes." I said, "I think I can do that." After that night he was on his way back to Philly the next day.

I still worked at Dolce Vita three days a week, and wanted another job. But I was content at that moment because now I had Paul as well.

I'm at work and it's time for my break. I went and got something to eat, and met this guy. He introduced himself by telling me his name is "D." Now, Paul and I weren't a couple. I wanted to be in a relationship with Paul, but he never said anything about making that happen. D was persistent in getting to know me. I still had Paul, but I gave D a chance only because he was here in Detroit, and Paul was in Philly.

D was from the east side of Detroit. Not street, but had a street way about him. One of our first dates was the strip club, "Chocolate City." This is my first time being in one, so I'm wondering why he wanted to take me there. He said, "We're going for the food." I laughed and said, "Okay." We saw some of D's other friends, and we really had a great time.

After a few days of dating D, I'm still trying to keep up with Paul, but keeping him in the dark about D, as he was still in Philly.

Paul finally came back to Detroit after two weeks. Even though we talked every day, it was nothing like seeing his face. Paul stood about five feet, eight inches tall, about 190 pounds, caramel-colored skin, with a chipped tooth and a small afro. I was so happy to see him!

I kept D at bay while Paul was in town. From the looks of it, it seemed like Paul was staying in town for a while because he came in with two large duffle bags. I thought he was getting ready to pull out some clothes. But to my surprise, he pulled out bundles and bundles of money with a money counter. I was in such shock, I just went in the other room.

Time went on that day. He called me back in the dining room to get him something to drink. As I looked down on the notes he had, as he counted, give or take there was about $385,000, and he was still counting. Now, that's when I got scared. I didn't know what Paul was into. He never told me. He truly kept me in the dark; but I knew it wasn't right.

The next day D is calling me, but I told him I had to work some more hours, and he was cool with that. He said he'll see me on the weekend. I felt at ease, as Paul wasn't leaving for a few more days. Later that day Paul and I went to a restaurant called Franklin's in downtown Detroit; a soul food place with a calm and elegant atmosphere.

We talked for over two hours, just truly getting to know each other. He asked me if I wanted to move to Philly. I couldn't say anything then. He asked again, saying, "I know we haven't been knowing each other that long, seven months to be exact, but I really want you and Tiana to come live with me." I said, "You don't really know me. Yes, we've slept together and talk every day, but you're never here consistently. Just back and forth from here to Philly. You've only seen Tiana twice. You don't know if she's a good kid or not."

I'm making good sense to him, but it's me using it for an excuse. I'm thinking to myself, "I'm young. I don't want to leave Detroit. What about my family: Doni, Lisa, Terrence, Jackie, everybody? I can't leave. Why can't it stay like this?!"

Paul was laying it on thick as he slid me an envelope with $10,000 in it and said, "You don't have to worry about nothin'! There's more where that came from if you'll just be with me." I told him, "I'll think about it."

As my Nextel phone was chirping (it was D), I turned it off and thought "I'll call D tomorrow." Paul and I had a great next two days of making love, going out to eat, and shopping. Then off he left with no definite answer from me if I was going to move with him. Paul was on his way back to Philly for about a week.

I called D, as I had lied to him, apologizing that I had to work more hours. He was fine with that. D's mind was on something else. I asked him what was wrong. He said, "Do you remember my friend Jeff Jones?" I said, "Yes." He said, "Someone killed Jeff." I was hurt for D as he bared the pain of his friend being murdered. Time went on and D wanted to spend a lot more time together, but I still had Paul around.

I grew scared, as I didn't want to lose D. Eventually, I moved in with D; and soon after, here comes Paul calling me saying it's too much going on. All he could say was he was extremely busy! I would sneak off to see Paul, but D was no fool. He found out about what I was doing, and threatened to put me out. Never hitting me then, but making it clear to stop seeing who I was seeing.

Paul drifted away. He tried to keep in touch. Eventually the calls just stopped. I was sad, but D filled the void. D worked in corporate America, so life was pretty good. His hustle and drive drove me to want to do more. He was in sales. They say in that business, "If you don't work, you don't eat!'"

D made a lot of money. But when sales were down, it affected our lifestyle. I didn't like it at all. I loved D, and was hurt that the money was not how it used to be.

One day D got a small commission check and we went to the mall. It was Hudson's at the time, and in the children's department they had these cute rabbit jackets in black and white. I saw the price and said, "I'm not paying for that. It's rabbit. A child's coat shouldn't cost that much."

I looked around, saw no one else was there, and took the white rabbit jacket for Tiana. D couldn't believe it.

I went back to the car and dropped off the coat and other items taken, and said, "I want the black one for her too." My adrenaline was on 1,000, and I was so bold to go back in and take the black one as well without getting caught. I was so excited to have gotten away with that, I wanted more.

Chapter 11
Taking Everything That's Mine

I was getting clothes left and right. I hit every store you could think of, from Neiman Marcus, to Walmart, from Lord and Taylor, to Sears. Any store in the United States you could think of, Tiffani hit that store in some way, shape, form, or fashion.

I was getting clothing for about six months. Then one day I took something back without a receipt. Back in the day, you could take things back without a receipt and get cash. Once I saw that, ideas set off in my head. I would hit the china department in Hudson's, and take back china, linen, and more. Anything pricey, I would take back because I knew they were going to give me cash. I did this for about two years, making a few hundred thousand dollars.

I worked this hustle like a job. I hit every store every day for about nine hours a day. The only time I stopped was when it was time to get Tiana from school. Sometimes I took her home to D, or sometimes she would be with me.

From cars, clothes, jewelry, whatever I wanted … I hustled hard to get it! Things I couldn't get out of Neiman's or Saks, I would just hustle and get the money to purchase what I wanted out of there.

At Tiana's school, the teachers asked her how many pairs of shoes and coats she had. The only reason I knew they asked that was because one day, I caught Tiana counting her shoes. You couldn't tell me nothin'! That's when I knew I was getting any and everything I wanted!

D and I grew tired of paying $2,000 a month on an apartment. Never knew we could build a home until we met this lady, Tracey, who lived across the hall from us and happened to be a loan officer. She hooked us up with a realtor that found us land to build on.

See, I couldn't put my illegal money in the bank to show it being seasoned, so D's job and his father's John Hancock (retirement money), helped us build our home in 1999. Breaking ground at 23, and D at 27-years-old, was major for us. I was on top of the world. None of my friends were living like me. I truly thought I was the "shit"!

As soon as we closed on the house, things changed in the stores. They weren't giving out money at the stores I was hitting anymore. The systems changed. I was so upset. We had a $1,600 mortgage, home insurance, car notes, car insurance, bills, other expenses that added up to almost $6,000 a month. All I could do was sit back and think about what was next. I don't know where the idea came from for my next move, but as time went on and years later, that was the final straw that landed me in prison in 2008.

By this time it's 2002. I've been to jail about five or six different times, but that didn't stop me. I'm doing my same method of looking like I could afford everything in the stores I walked into. I would hustle in mink coats, hair done, jewelry, and driving good, so the people who worked in the stores would compliment me, say I looked nice, and not label me a thief.

When I went into Neiman Marcus, Saks, and Jacobson's, I looked like I was supposed to be there, and the same for the other stores. I've already been convicted for some of those stores, that's why I can talk about them so freely.

I always worked by myself. Not having a partner in my crimes worked best for me, as I never wanted to get into trouble and have someone tell on me, making it worse. I used to wish at the time I had someone by my side to help because I would be so tired from driving all the time, going from store to store all day long.

I was working my hustle so hard that D and I began to drift apart. I started to look at D in a different light. I did respect him as a man, but didn't respect that I was making so much more money than him. He couldn't take care of Tiana and I, so that made it hard for me to stay in a relationship with him, even though I loved him and wanted things to work. We tried to overcome the lack of money he brought in, but eventually it tore us apart.

See, here goes God again, stepping in, moving me on from one lesson to another when it came to a man. Now, I know God hated what I was doing to get money, but it made me grow as a woman to not depend on a man for financial gain.

Paul did everything for Tiana and I. I didn't put everything in this book. It somewhat made me want to get the kind of money he was getting, but not from drugs and money laundering. God got me away from Paul because I could have gotten into the drug game. God took me away from D, as I could have let what I was doing get worse and take us both under.

Thank you, God, for life's lessons, and removing me from weak situations; doing so, made me more independent and strong. God was keeping me and covering me. I didn't know it then like I know now.

Chapter 12
The Worst Man I Ever Had

It's late 2003. I met my husband; we'll just call him "AP." AP wasn't a street nor corporate guy. He was a guy who talked a good game; blinded me by his talk of who he knew and where he said he could take me in life. Now remember, I loved D. I even loved Paul. But, I was vulnerable because D and I were on the rocks, about to split up, Paul was in another state, so AP wiggled his way right on in.

As I tell the story about AP, I will say that God was looking out for me in that time of being with AP; another man that I would take care of, get him out of trouble, take care of him like he was my child of sorts -- forgave him for all the disrespect, the women, the lies, the drinking, the gambling, the staying out all night, the fights, and the arguing. And with all that being said, AP "knew God," but I promise he was the devil in disguise.

I had to learn hard dealing with AP. How could I love a man so much who treated me so badly? It's late 2003, and, boy, did AP sweep me off my feet with his lies. Dealing with AP took me from one extreme to another. He was a traveling church musician. So I would pick him up from the airport and take him, not to his home, but to his mother's house. That was a red flag. He made me believe his condo caught fire and that's why he was living at his mom's house temporarily.

Now, I still had another man on the side who I would see from time to time. Let's talk about him first, as I had great memories with him. Good ol' "Denim." Talk about having so much fun with someone who was MARRIED, but would hang with me, pay my bills, and have me around his wife. I would stay quiet about our relationship because I thought I loved him so much, I didn't want to be "disrespectful" towards his wife.

I put a car in my name for Denim, not realizing that he took this car home to his family. Letting him store drugs at my condo because he didn't dare take them home to his family. Hell, Denim was cheating on me and his wife with other women. I was so young and such a fool. Denim was a fun and exciting guy to be around, but I never knew other things he had going on in the street would make me feel sad and have his family in my thoughts and prayers all the time.

AP came along, and I was ready for my three-month romance with Denim to end. Denim was murdered in 2003.

AP now has talked me into moving. Not around the corner or down the street, or even to another suburb, but to Florida. Here I go saying I wouldn't have my daughter around the men in my life. And here I go ready to move us to Florida with him. Tiana hated him, even at nine years old. She told me she didn't like AP, and didn't want me with him.

We moved to Florida. I gave up everything except my clothes and Tiana's clothing. We only stayed there a month or so, came back, and moved to one of his grandmother's properties; and life as we know it went downhill when I was with him.

We then moved from his grandmother's property to an apartment that I paid for. Hell, I paid for everything, and I wasn't used to this. What was I thinking being with this man? Brainwashed for love that I wasn't getting. I had family who loved me, but wanted no part of me if I was with him. My cousin Danielle would get so mad at me for being with him, knowing I could do so much better.

By late 2003, I was pregnant with our first child. But because AP was doing so many disrespectful things to me, I didn't want to bring another child into the world, so I had an abortion. AP knew I was pregnant, and was upset I had an abortion. But that was my way of getting back at him.

My cousins, Danielle and Toya, were so happy, knowing that I didn't need to have a baby by that bum. But I stayed. I didn't listen to my cousins. And by early 2004, I had gotten pregnant again and kept this one. That made me go into overdrive with my hustle. I had a baby coming. I hustled while pregnant. Went to jail a few times pregnant, and still didn't stop.

See, AP was a man that loved working in the church as a minister of music. His father, being a pastor and all, made me love being a part of that family. His father taught us about God; how to do right. And despite our mistakes, God will never give up on you. I think after a while I wanted to be with that part of the family, but not AP.

In March 2004, AP and I went to Ohio and got married. Why? I can't tell you, but I know his mother, father, and stepmother played a part. I loved them and thought that maybe they could help me change him. I didn't want to bring another child into the world out of wedlock.

October 29, 2004, I had a beautiful seven-pound-ten-ounce baby boy, and I named him Allen Michael Peak. I thought my son coming to us was going to change everything and make things better, but it didn't. The fighting grew. AP's other women were disrespectful. His staying out all night and gambling got worse.

I made up what we would lose to his gambling with my hustling. AP would always apologize and want me to take him back after I would put him out. He would beg to come back. And me being a fool, would let him back in, have sex, and here I go again, pregnant, having Alexander Cole Peak in March of 2006. Then, eleven months later, March of 2007, I had Blake Austin Peak.

Now, at this time I was hustling harder than ever. I was married to a real working bum. I was going to church, tithing and paying my offerings with my illegal money. Yes, I said paying my tithes with my illegal money. AP would get paid from his church gigs, going from church to church, and not bringing a dime back home. So I'm paying for everything!

His gambling got so bad ... Let's say I made about six to eight thousand dollars that week, and hid it in the house. I promise he would find it and spend it. On what? I don't know. Maybe his women on the side, gambling, drinking? I don't know. When I went to my hiding spot to get my money, it would be gone.

The drinking would get so bad that we would fight. Sometimes if his other women didn't let him in to stay with them, he would sleep in the car. And when I would let him back in, there was more drama!

The last straw was on a Sunday night, going into Monday morning. It was about 2:00 a.m., and I'm calling AP's cell. No answer when it rang. And after about 3:00 a.m., it went dead. AP would get careless and stupid. I knew he was out drunk somewhere; I just didn't know where. I called his mother, Ann, and all she said was, "You know how he is. He'll be home."

AP was so disrespectful! He wouldn't call home or anything. He was a mess to me and our household, but I never wanted anything to happen to him. He was careless. Yeahp! I had the passcode to his phone. Hell, I was paying the bill.

I checked his voicemail and I wasn't surprised to hear a woman's voice saying, "I thought you were on your way. Then you call me and say you had a flat tire. I keep calling you and your phone is going straight to the voicemail. Ooh, you make me sick!" I hung up the phone. That woman sounded like me.

I knew what I had to do next, and that was to prepare to leave AP. I called his mother again and I played the message, and she couldn't say a word. I sat in the basement on the sofa waiting on him so I could beat his ass with whatever I got my hands on. I could always beat AP because he would be so drunk, he couldn't lift a finger.

It's 4:00 a.m., and I hear my doorbell ring. Every house I've ever lived in, I've never had blinds, and my drapes were always drawn back even at night. So as I came up the stairs, I looked out my living room window and I see some woman banging on my door. It was nobody but God, because I couldn't open my heavy door. Our locks were done in the opposite direction.

So I'm pumped to open the door, but can't! She ran off our porch and drove off into the night. I was pissed by now. I called his mother again. Now she's mad. I was a good daughter-in-law, and she knew it.

I got off the phone with my mother-in-law after about twenty minutes. I called his voicemail, and of course, there's a new message. It's the woman that was at the front door going off on him, calling him a liar, saying, "You not even at home. Your car is not there." THAT WAS IT! I WAS DONE!

When AP came home, it was time for me to take Tiana to school. I told myself I wasn't going to argue with him. I just had a plan to leave him in the gutter where he belonged. He came strolling in smelling like cheap liquor, and I went about my day.

When I came back home, he didn't understand why I wasn't saying anything; not arguing or fighting with him. So he got upset and threw a closed beer can at me and it hit my shoulder. I picked up every vase, book, lamp, chair -- everything I could get my hands on, I threw at him until I got close to him, and he knocked me clear across the floor. That's it! He left. I packed all of his clothes and set them

73

outside like trash. I didn't want our neighbors to think we're a bunch of ghetto-fighting fools, but I had to do it.

About four days went by, and here he comes back in. By that time, I had found a house to lease in Southfield, Michigan. I had to get my children out of this horrible environment. He saw me packing that next week or so, and really thought we were still going to be together.

We never talked about the night the woman came by, and the huge fight we had that left my beautiful home in shambles. But I didn't care. My motto was: "I bought it once, I can buy it again."

We sat in the kitchen and I did ask him, "Why and what, I'm not good enough for you?" I told him that I heard the voicemail messages, and I even talked with the woman. I was talking so calmly, he couldn't believe it was me. He got scared and stayed away a few more days. Maybe he thought I was going to kill him. I wasn't. I had a plan.

May 2008

I'm planning to leave my husband at the time. I'm just tired of all the turmoil that's going on in our relationship. So I'm hustling harder than ever to pick up and leave with my children. I figured out a way to get cash money again. I had friends that did the "credit card and checks" scheme, but I knew that came with federal time, so I never tried it.

I took the "small way" to make a lot of money. I've been convicted from these stores, so I can talk freely about it. Marshalls, TJ Maxx, and Home Goods were my go to, to get the cash. I would take things from the store of good value, and made sure they would give me a store credit. I would then take that store credit, buy something of equal value, and then change the receipt to cash.

I know you're saying how did I do that? I would take the receipt and wipe off the SVC part of the receipt with perfume because the perfume had alcohol in it, and it wiped away what was on the receipt that I didn't want on there. Then I would take a cash receipt and use transparent tape to lift up the word cash to place on the SVC receipt, then tape the receipt to the item and take it back to the store to get the money.

That was a daily routine. I worked this hustle like a 12-hour shift until I got tired, except on Sundays, because I had to go to church and pay my tithes and offerings. I was crooked, but tried to have morals. Go figure!

I love God, and giving my children the best life, lifestyle, and all that they need. I wish I had went to college. All the work I put into corrupting the system, I could have poured that into a corporation, learning to be a doctor or so much more. But I chose to do this, and it cost me almost everything.

I would hit these stores so hard that it got to a point they were watching me, wondering who I was. Thinking I've worked there in the past, not knowing if I had others working with me or for me. I was working so hard to purchase another home to get away from my husband at the time, that I got arrogant and cocky, thinking I was invincible because the money was coming so fast.

June 2008

It's bill time all over again like any other month. So I did what I did best – hit the stores. I didn't let Tiana go to school that day. I had her with me. I just needed a few thousand real quick, but that was short-lived.

I went to TJ Maxx to get back about $600, and when I left out the store, I saw this man walking fast behind me. I brushed it off. He got in a car. I said to myself, "no one is behind me, " so I pulled off.

Shortly after, we pulled into McDonald's and as soon as we left, West Bloomfield Police were behind me, ripping me out of my truck, searching my truck for more items and/or evidence; And there it was, my paper trail.

I used to clean my truck out all the time just in case I did get pulled over, nothing would be in there. Not this time. They used everything against me when I got to court.

My husband was no help. Never got me out of jail or anything. It felt like payback for spoiling my kids, doing more than he did. I couldn't believe out of all the money I made, I looked up and had nothing. He took it all. I sat in jail. Never got bonded out by him, nor did he even try. I truly thought I was coming home. I finally gave up.

The charges against me were First Degree Retail Fraud, First Degree Child Endangerment, and Second Degree Uttering and Publishing. Now, I understand the first two charges, but didn't understand Uttering and Publishing. I thought that was pushing checks, which I never did.

The detective told me when I was signing my name to receive fraudulent money, that was "uttering and publishing."

I'm still not thinking I would get a lot of time, but I was already on probation from 2004, therefore, it wasn't looking good for me in court.

Chapter 13
Time to Go

August 2008

I'm before Judge Rudy J. Nichols in the Oakland County Circuit Court, 1200 North Telegraph Road, Pontiac, Michigan. It's sentencing day. I'm thinking they would honor what my lawyer suggested and give me a year in jail (that's really about ten months in jail.) That day, Judge Nichols was sending everyone to prison. But, I thought differently as the Judge began to talk to me.

He said, "Mrs. Peak, so you understand the charges against you, and you've pled guilty before the Court?" I said, "Yes, your Honor."

"Mrs. Peak, you said you had no one working with you?" I said, "No!"

He said, "You did all of this by yourself?" I said, "Yes!"

"Well, Mrs. Peak, Mrs. Bell (Bell is my maiden name), whatever your name is, you're just a one-woman crime spree! You have children, and this is what you chose to do. You robbed these stores blind. We have on paper that you took $367,384.17 in cash and merchandise from these companies. We know it's more, but the Prosecutor hasn't presented more proof. Is there anything you'd like to say before the Court?"

"Your Honor, I apologize to the Court, but I never did it to live a glamorous lifestyle (lying). I did it for my children, to provide for them (truth).

But what did I say that for? He said, "Okay. I don't want to hear anymore. I hereby sentence you to 18 months in the MDOC" (Michigan Department of Corrections). But later turned into two years because another store came and prosecuted as well. I WAS DEVASTATED!

I looked over at my lawyer and said, "I thought you said a year in jail! What's the MDOC?" I knew it was prison, I just wanted to hear him say it. He looked off and said, "PRISON," Michigan Department of Corrections." They whisked me off as I looked at my family who were in disbelief, tears, and sad.

My cycle was over. I didn't see my family for two years. That's not a lot of time. Looking at everything I've done in eighteen years of hustling and getting over on the system, scheming, scamming, and being fraudulent in these stores that I've made over $1,000,000 from -- two years was a true slap on the wrist! Everything I've done should have given me twenty years. But even in that time, GOD WAS COVERING ME!

I traveled, bought homes, cars, took care of others, paid folks' rent, car notes, took care of my children, paid for abortions for friends that the men they slept with wouldn't pay for, partied – you name it, I had done it all!

My family called me the modern day Robin Hood: "rob the rich to give to the poor." I even took care of a few men in my past. What a loser in so many ways! I put my hustle before my children, and it almost cost me a relationship with them. I left a fourteen-year-old teenage daughter, a three-year-old son with autism, a two-year-old son, and a thirteen-month-old baby boy. I was so mad at myself that I couldn't even cry. If you know me, imagine that! I knew I was wrong, and I was ready to take on my punishment.

A few days after sentencing, I arrived at "The Big House," as they called it, "Scotts Women's Correctional Facility." (It's torn down now.) This place is gigantic. Intimidated by all the different-looking women that at that time I didn't know were women, I asked someone, "I thought this was a women's prison." They said, "It is." Some of the women looked like men. They called them "studs."

Now, I have nothing against homosexuals. I had just never been around women who looked like men. Because some women had long sentences, they ultimately chose to just be with women; something I didn't understand.

In prison, you see a lot when they call you out for a healthcare run. I mean, a lot: passing/smuggling items (so the correctional officers wouldn't see), sex in the showers, recreational drugs, liquor, and so much more!

I had to stay in quarantine for 60 days. Well, all of us did – those that were coming into prison from the outside world. Locked down twenty-three hours a day, waiting for all of your test results to come back: TB test, AIDS, sexually transmitted infections – you name it, the tests got ran.

After that, you could go on the grounds. I had to make the best of it. Prison was a world inside of a world. I just wanted to find my friend Ri and a lady named Anna. Ri, I knew from home. Anna was someone I got cool with as we sat in jail. I just wanted to be around familiar people.

Because prison wasn't familiar to me, I grew depressed thinking about my children, not being able to call home yet. But as soon as I was able to call home, wow! If prison wasn't bad enough, that first call I made home wasn't good.

I called my friend Tiki (now deceased). She said, "Tiffani, I just went and got Tiana. AP jumped on Tiana real bad! He beat her so bad, she had bruises on her." I was pissed. AP would not have pulled that shit if I was home. All because of her talking to a boy on the phone. "Really," is what I was thinking.

That was me he was beating, except it was my daughter. A bum, nothing-ass bum jumped on my baby. I was so weak and helpless because I couldn't do anything but sign power of attorney over to my friend for my daughter.

My mother-in-law had my boys. She was good to them, and I appreciated her for that! But Tiana wasn't her granddaughter, so it was best that Tiana went with Tiki, then later on with my adopted sister Lisa.

My family were doing their part to take care of my kids, so I focused on me, my thought process, and how I was going to change when I got home after my two years were up.

I'm on grounds in my housing unit. My crime was low in prison, so I was a Level 1. I had thirteen bunkies in prison (roommates/cellmates) in my two years; maybe more. I was moved around so much I couldn't find my friend until after my second move to another unit, and there was my friend Ri with two other ladies. I was so happy to see someone I knew. It was a lot going on at home, that it was cool to talk about back home, our past, and what our future was going to be when we got home.

I was happy to be given a cleaning job that paid eight dollars a month. Eight dollars... how could I live off of that? See, I owed restitution, so whatever money my mother-in-law or my good girlfriend Boo would send, the prison or State would only let me get the first thirty dollars. So every month, no matter how much was sent to me, I only got thirty dollars plus the eight dollars. What was I going to do with that?

I would see people passing stuff, smuggling things around, and I wanted to do the same; but I needed product of some sort, or so I thought. My friend Ri did hair back home, owned a salon, did real estate, a mortgage company – you name it, she owned it.

Ri taught me a skill in prison so I could make money. She taught me how to razor cut the white women's hair. I already knew how to style hair on black women, but razor cutting white women's wet hair was in demand.

I started making money to buy things from the "store," and obtained products to buy other products from inmates (barter).

I cut and styled hair. I arched eyebrows. Yes, eyebrows. Ri taught me how to break down razors so I could arch eyebrows and cut hair. She looked out for me so I could afford anything from Ramen noodles to gym shoes, underwear, and more.

By this time, it's five of us hanging together. Women with a short amount of time to do – we were just ready to go home.

I went to my friends and told them, "You know cigarettes are being taken out of the prison." My Bunkie told me I can make a killing on selling them once they take them off the store sheet. We all didn't smoke, so I wasn't worried about the product getting smoked up before we could sell it. It was time to hustle.

By the time cigarettes got out of the prison in February of 2009, I was selling pouches of cigarettes for $100.00, and single rollups for $10.00. I was feeling so good to be making this small money. It was like being a millionaire in prison.

Trying to make the time go by in prison took a lot of imagination. Wondering what you were going to do when you got home, as things changed, people changed, and so much more.

All I could do was imagine the good things that were going to happen when I stepped outside those prison doors. I had two years to do, so by now, the time I had left, I made the best of it with my friends I had there.

Prison

A world inside of a world, like a big college campus. But, you stayed in your lane in there because anyone could not like you because of some of the stupidest reasons.

You're around 2,000 women, so what do you expect? Childishness, negativity, jealousy, hate, and not knowing if this person is cool or not, or just trying to use you, set you up, or get over on you. I've seen it all. That's why I liked my lil' click I was around.

After about two months, the Level 1's are getting ready to get shipped off to Camp White Lake. Boy, were we excited. They say it's better to go to the camp than the prison.

I thought it was better at the camp. The camp ran itself like the prison, but not locked down as much, except for a few counts. That statewide count at 3:00 p.m., OMG, it would take over an hour to count all of the prisoners in Michigan. It seemed like forever.

I know it sounds crazy for me to say this, but we made the best of our times there. Not happy, but just made the best of it.

I had two situations with two women; a career criminal named Val -- A fat, ugly, gay-for-the-stay type broad. Yes, I said gay-for-the-stay! She had another chick take care of her because she had nothing. And, she was always starting something.

I was 220 pounds when I got to prison. Hell, I wanted to lose weight before I went home, and I did extreme things to do just that. I didn't eat in the chow hall, but would go if it was certain things I wanted. I drank a lot of water, and even did a "popcorn diet." It worked. I would get laxatives from the nurse just so I could shit the weight off. You name it, Ri and I did it to lose weight.

Val was so into what I was doing, she told the correctional officers on me. I thought that was the craziest thing. She would come up to me and say, "You not eating today, or you just gon' drink your juice?" I'm like, "Why you worried about me losing weight?" She's like, "I'm just saying." So I told her, "I'ma say this to you, bitch. Don't worry about me. Take notes, bitch, and lose some of that fat off of you!" I turned away, and she pushed me into the wall.

This was the stupidest reason to have a fight, but I did. Not worried about the cameras in our unit, I beat that fat bitch's ass. Everyone was happy because she was the messiest chick in the unit. She told people she was going to set me up. Others that thought I was cool told her not to do that. I never spoke to her again, even though this next lady I'm about to tell y'all about got involved and made her apologize to me.

S.B. was a woman who had natural life at first, but her sentence got overturned, and she only did 22 years. S.B. was cool, but scary and creepy in a way. We heard so many stories about her; why she was there, and what she'll do to you if you crossed her while in prison. In our minds, we were no match for Ms. Barker (S.B.). S.B. was with women before we got there. But by the time she would be around us, she became focused on herself trying to get home. So, she had no relationship with a woman. She would just stay to herself or come around us.

Time has gone by, months, even a year. We're getting closer to going home. And, for whatever reason, someone told S.B. I said something about her. We're in the yard, and she asked me did I. I said, "Yeah, I think you're the devil, and I don't want to be around you like the others do." So I walked away pissed because the person who told her was this nothing-ass bitch named T.T. She didn't like me, and I didn't like her. But Ri did, so I went along with it.

S.B. came up to me and said, "Why would you say that about me?" I said, "Get the fuck out my face!" She slapped me across the face! Boy, was I pissed. I wanted to beat her ass so badly, but I didn't want to go to segregation, and I had months to go before I would go home. I just didn't want them to take my parole from me, so I ate that slap up.

She later apologized and said she understood why I felt the way I did, and let's just focus on going home. I accepted her apology. Folks thought I was crazy, but I just wanted to go home.

Once I was released, S.B. did reach out to me while I was sick with cancer, and apologized again. Not for the prison incident, but because I was sick. I told her, "Girl, I'm fine. I thought you were apologizing for prison, because I just want you to know that prison shit don't work out here with me. If we were here and you did that, I would have beat your ass!" She laughed when I said that, but I was serious. I did eventually laugh it off, but I just wanted her to know that the Tiffani from prison was the Tiffani that wanted to go home and had something to lose. The Tiffani in the streets would have let her have it!

Prison was one crazy environment that I wouldn't wish my worst enemy to go to. From Scotts Correctional, to Camp White Lake, back to Huron Valley Correctional, that's a time of headache and bullshit I'll never forget!

See, God was prepping me and my friends in that hell hole. It could have been different. I could have gotten caught up in a web of hurt and mess that would have kept me away from my family even longer.

So, thank you, God, for keeping me and my friends away from the drugs, homosexuality, and the crooked correctional officers not raping or bothering us like they did others. And the little mess I did have going on, thank you for covering me.

I didn't know God was keeping me then, but I know now!

Chapter 14
Home Again

February 16, 2010

It's time to go home. My Aunt Veta and Cousin Danielle were right there to pick me up. I was ready. No more petty, jealous women, or walking the track to make time go by, working out, eating bold food, drinking well water, working for pennies, and most of all, not seeing my family.

Oh, what a joy to see my family! Tiana, Allen Michael, Alexander, and Blake. Blake didn't know who I was. He's my youngest, and was only 13 months when I left. He would cry and fall out because he didn't know me, and surely didn't want to come with me. I got so mad, I told my mother-in-law, "You can have him. I'm not going to deal with a child who doesn't want to come with me."

I was so mad at myself because my baby boy didn't know me. Asking myself, "What have I done?" He needs to know I'm his mother, not his aunt, not his grandmother or great-grandmother, but me!

I talked to my sister and niece, Lisa and Doni, and they told me, "Don't take 'no' for an answer. That's your child!" I listened and did just that. I kept Blake with me all the time, building my love with him. My other children were fine. They loved me, and nothing else mattered. Blake grew to love me more and more. And now, years later, you can't keep us apart.

God was always there. I could have lost all of the love from my children, but God didn't allow that to happen. My bond with my four children is stronger than ever before.

April 2010

I'm home a few months from prison. I have a male friend who allowed me to stay at one of his rental properties. I took advantage of that because I had paroled to my mother-in-law's house, and I was ready to leave from there.

I'm looking around and I have my children with me. My mother-in-law bought me a dining room set and the boys' beds. The guy I'm with, who we'll call "T", had given me a bed, washer, dryer, refrigerator, and stove, but it still wasn't enough. I was grateful, but triggers were setting off in my head, and I wanted more. My family didn't know at the time, but I'm fresh out of prison, hustling again. Here I go, back to the same thing. I just can't stop.

I'm spoiling Tiana, trying to make up for what was lost. I lost everything when I got sent to prison. The only things I had were some coats, two Rolex watches, a few pieces of jewelry, and a box of old family pictures. I LOST EVERYTHING!

I went into a hustle mode that was better this time than before I went to prison, or so I thought. See, my family, Lisa and Doni, tried to adopt me when Tiana was about three. A few years later I told Doni, "I didn't sign the papers because I didn't want y'all to know all the corrupt, illegal, bad things I was doing;" and I didn't want their names attached to me.

See, family knows when you're right and wrong. My family knew I was back to my old ways. Not even home from prison six months, and here I go again. I tried to hide it, but they knew.

By August 2010, I had enough money to get another car because I was driving one of T's cars. I had money for a townhouse. I was just waiting to sign the lease and move in. I had a house full of furniture and clothes for my children. I knew I was taking a chance, but I was trying to get my family back "right."

By December 2010, I'm closing on a condo in the "WB" (West Bloomfield), as we called it. I'm back on Cloud 9. Not home from prison a year, and I'm in my ideal neighborhood, thanks to my friends who are realtors, Ri from prison, and her husband Mont. I'm doing good. We're a family and comfortable ... until 2012. This is the year of my daughter's prom and graduation. Oh boy!

I want to pull out all the stops! I want a Rolls Royce, $3,000 Louboutin shoes for her, this $1,000 dress, a Glam Squad, a helicopter, and a food spread for everyone that's coming over. I wanted the glam life for my child at its finest. But as I'm getting the money together, everything changed.

It's May 23, 2012, the day before Tiana's prom. I'm out getting the last money needed for what was planned out. I've been convicted by this store, so I can talk freely about it. Von Maur reminds you of Nordstrom or Jacobson's, if you can remember Jacobson's from back in the day. That was one of my go-to's to get money.

There were only two stores in Michigan, but I didn't care. I worked them hard.

See, let me tell y'all something about God. He was keeping me, even in this situation. The store had turned me away twice on that Wednesday before, but I didn't care. I kept pushing it. That was God speaking to me; telling me, "Tiffani, let it go," but I didn't listen. I kept going.

So as I ignored God, I went out the next day (the day before her prom) and tried again. Sure enough, this store had been watching me too. And as I was leaving, here comes Loss Prevention yelling and screaming. I had Tiana and Blake with me that day, and I yelled I had a gun. See, that "I had a gun" thing worked in the past, and I got away with it. So I thought I could do it again. IT DIDN'T WORK!

They took me away that day, and the charges against me were not good: First Degree Unarmed Robbery carries 15 to 20 years; First Degree Retail Fraud, two to five years; First Degree Child Endangerment, one to five years. I was done!

I'm sitting in jail, knowing my bond was going to be high as the sky. Look, I'm a five-time felon, a habitual offender in the second degree, and I know that no Judge will set me free on a low bond; not with my background.

Oh, But God

It's May 24, 2012; Tiana's prom day. Nothing was accomplished for her. No helicopter, no car, the prom dress wasn't finished being paid for, hair not done, and I'm going to miss her going to prom. But again, it's nothing greater than being covered by a God who loves you in all of your faults.

I went before the Magistrate via video court, and I explained to him that "today is my daughter's prom. I understand the charges against me, and I'll take them head-on. But, please, let me see my daughter go off to prom."

I just knew he was going to say $20,000, $50,000 or even $100,000 for a bond. But by the grace of God, he said $15,000/10% (which is $1,500). I could have passed out. I said to myself, "They can pawn one of my Rolex watches." I was so happy, but disgusted with myself, all at the same time. What a fool! I was in trouble again, all because I wanted this big prom send-off. The key words, "I wanted..."

See, Tiana never wanted anything I've ever given her. She received it, but that was never a child who wanted the latest everything. That was all me. She just liked new phones and cute clothes. Nothing major. I knew I had disappointed her, but she was glad I was there.

The best thing that came out of all of this was the day she graduated from high school on June 3, 2012. I had so much going on, but God allowed me to see her make it across the stage at her gradation.

I was so determined to run away from this case, that I moved myself and the kids to Atlanta. I really thought they were going to transfer things down there, but I had to fly back and forth to fight the case.

I had one attorney (court appointed), but I fired him quickly. I needed to have a "good" attorney. The charges against me were First Degree Unarmed Robbery, etc. I couldn't have an officer of the court represent me. I didn't know where the money was going to come from, but something had to happen in my favor.

August 2012

My friend Shell called me and said that our friend Kelli and some of her male friends she grew up with were coming to Atlanta. I was so excited, as I was missing home and worried about my case I had going on back there.

It was a breath of fresh air when they got there. Shell introduced me to the guys. Of course, I already knew Shell and Kelli. The crew was Jack, RaRu, John, Turf, Lamont, and Rick. We all clicked, as it was Jack's, Roshelle's, and Rick's birthday month.

At that time we're with a bunch of men, and where did they want to go? To the strip club, Onyx Strip Club. It's a Thursday night, not that crowded. But, boy, did our first encounter of meeting each other end up leading to a huge fight. Not between us, but us against the strippers. It was crazy.

It's three women and six men against nine strippers, two male managers, and security. It was crazy. We fought our way out of there! If the guys weren't there, we would have gotten killed by those strippers.

I got hit in the head with a Moet bottle, Roshelle's hair got pulled out, and Kelli twisted her ankle. The guys were beating the crap out of the women to get them off of us. It was crazy. But for some strange reason, when we got to the hospital to check my head and Kelli's ankle, we just laughed!

The next day we ate at The Cheesecake Factory and talked about the night before. From that day forward, I was their "honorary Lil' Sister." I guess the respect that they had for me getting down and dirty, kicking, fighting, breaking bottles and all, and we didn't even know each other, made them look at me like, "She's cool. She can hang with us!" The weekend was over and it's time for them to go. We all got each other's numbers, and they've been here for me ever since.

Pressure for me to come back to Michigan is at an all-time high. I had nowhere to go when I got back to Detroit. I could have went to my family, but my pride was too strong to ask if I could come to them. Tiana is now at Michigan State, so it's just my three sons and I.

I had been talking with one of the guys a lot, nothing sexual. He would give me advice, just really being a big brother. I told him I had to come back, and asked did he have something for me to rent, or did the other guys have something.

RaRu told me he had a spot; a little honeycomb hideout, as he called it. RaRu gave me the address. I packed myself and the boys up, got a U-Haul, and on I-75 we go, leaving Atlanta, going back to Detroit. When I arrived in Detroit and pulled up to the house RaRu had on Derby Street, it was truly something I wasn't used to. But I had better not complain because I didn't have a pot to piss in, or a window to throw it out of!

RaRu welcomed me with open arms, saying, "It's not much, but it's yours for a week." That week grew into three months. RaRu never complained. I kept the house clean. The boys were in order. And money, wow, I truly don't know how I really had money, but it was there. Not a lot, but it was there.

The guys had really taken me under their wings. Maybe they felt sorry for me; a single mother in trouble, and no help with her three sons. Jack would come by and give me money. Lamont was always feeding the boys and I, and giving me money. Rick always said, "Whatever you need ... just call both my phones." And when I needed him, Rick was right there. They all were. No matter how big or small, they all were right there!

We ran the streets, partying, shopping, and doing things we truly had no business doing. But in doing so, we didn't bother anybody, and nobody bothered us. Roshelle and the guys would come over on Derby Street and keep me company, ease my mind because I didn't know how I was going to get out of the mess I was in.

October 23, 2012

It's my birthday. Roshelle, RaRu, and the whole crew planned a surprise birthday party at a club called PV for me. I was so surprised. I started crying in the club.

As the night went on, Jack and a few of his friends started showering me with money. All you could hear Jack saying was, "That's not enough. Give her more." That went on for about ten minutes. When they stopped showering me with money, Roshelle gathered it up and counted $8,200. I really cried!

The guys said, "Look, Tiffani, if you go to jail, don't call us for no commissary money." All I could do was laugh and cry at the same time. I couldn't believe it. I truly felt the love from friends that I've only known for a few months. Not because of the money, but because they had myself and my sons' best interest at heart.

That money gave me a kick-start to get an apartment and move out of the drug-infested neighborhood on Derby Street; having my children in a more secure and safe environment.

One of my friends helped me. She was always there when I needed her, big sister "M." I just didn't want to owe her a lot of money, but she was there.

One night my big sis M asked me to go to this party with her; a place called Hazel's Place. We're having a good time, and this guy came up to me and said, "My mans over there in the corner wants to holla at you." I said, "Holla? That's not how he can get my attention."

He went back and told him that. So he sends the bartender to me and said, "Please take this drink. He gave me $100 to bring this to you. And if you don't take it, I have to give it back." We both laughed. I said, "Okay." M said, "Please, say something to him."

I walked over to the heavy-set, almost 400-pound, dark-skinned man dressed plain, but clean. He said, "Hey, Baby Girl, I likes you." I said, "Likes me? Please go on somewhere." He laughed and said, "You don't know who I am?" I said, "No." He said, "Oh, you'll find out." I said, "Okay. Whatever you say."

He said, "What are you doing when you leave here?" I said, "Going home." He told me, "How about you and your girl come with me to the Vegas Strip Club down the street? They have a booth ready for me when we get there." Still not knowing his name, I told my friend M, "I don't want to go." She's like, "Come on!"

We get to the strip club, and he has ten guys with him. So we just followed behind them and went right in. They sat us right down in a booth, and here come the bottles. I felt like I was in the movie "Goodfellas." The part when Henry took Karen on their first date, and the restaurant pulled out all the stops for them; Except, we were in a strip club. See, God has His way of putting people in your life for a season and reason.

Big Mick was his name; a man that asked me what I did in the daytime. I said, "What you mean? As far as work? I don't work. I'm trying not to go back to prison," is what I told him! He said, "Prison?" I said, "Yes. I'm trying to build the money up to pay for this lawyer, Otis Culpepper." He said, "What you need to give him?" I said, "$8,500." He's like, "That's no problem. I don't want you to go to jail before I get to know you. Bump into me tomorrow, and I'll give you the money."

"Look at God," is all I thought. I didn't even have the money in my hand, but he made me cry in the club. "I just met him," asking God when I got home, "Why me?" But I didn't get too excited. I had to calm down. Men can promise you things and break that promise. So I went about my night and waited for his call the next day.

It's Football Sunday. He did tell me he would be watching the game and would call me afterwards. He called me late that night, but not to give me the money to take to Mr. Culpepper on Monday. He was apologizing that he went all day without hooking up with me to give me the money. I said, "It's okay." But in the back of my mind I'm saying, "This is some bullshit!" He then told me he'll see me in the morning before I go see my lawyer at 11:00 a.m. I just said, "Okay," and hung up the phone.

It's Monday, and my friend Shell and I went to this restaurant called Connie & Barbra's to eat breakfast before I went to see Mr. Culpepper. We're eating and talking, and she asked me, "Has he called yet?" I said, "No!" She said, "Call him." I told her, "I don't want to look pressed." She said, "You are pressed." So I called Mick, but he was calling me at the same time. So I just played it off like he called me.

He said, "Hey, Baby Girl, where you at?" I told him, where I was, but that I was getting ready to leave. He said, "I'm not coming in. Sit right there. I'll be there in fifteen minutes to bring you the money!" I said, "Okay," and hung up! I looked at Shell in disbelief and said, "he's really coming." She said, "Girl, well, let's wait."

I see a black Escalade turn the corner with Mick in the driver's seat. He caught my attention and gestured for me to come get in the truck. I gave him a hug as he began to pull out stacks of 20's, 50's, and 100 dollar bills, totaling $9,000. I said, "All I needed was $8,500." He said, "Give him nine so he's guaranteed to win the case."

I was so emotional I couldn't even cry. All I could say was, "Thank you, thank you, thank you," and hugged him so tight. He had to go, so I kissed him on the cheek and exited the Escalade. He pulled off. All Roshelle could say was, "Don't talk to me. Go! Go! You've got a case to win!"

See, I looked at God in so many ways. First as a provider, a healer, a coverer, a deliverer, a comforter, and a Spirit that can place people in your life when you need them. Not so much financially, but spiritually.

Mick was a street guy from the eastside of Detroit, but knew and knows God. When we talked about what he did for me, he told me, "God placed me in your life for a reason. No matter if you did wrong or not, no woman should be away from their children." I told Mick I was wrong, and I'm going to pay for it hard this time. Mick said, "I'm not going to let that happen. You're mine now, and I'm going to make sure everything is handled so you won't have to see another jail cell."

Mick showered my children and I with money and gifts. We even took a trip to Chicago to send off one of his friends who was going to prison in a few months. And, boy, did we shop!

It's right before Christmas, so the Magnificent Mile in Chicago was my friend. Mick's driver and friend drove us around from store to store. When I came out, they were right there waiting on me. Mick never went in the stores, he just sat in the truck and waited.

I woke up the next morning in our hotel room with four caret diamond earrings, two carets each ear. I don't know how Mick did it; he was with me the whole time. I'm assuming he sent someone to get them.

I was too outdone. Big Mick! My big black teddy bear was doing everything to make me happy.

Mick had a lot on his mind due to the feds coming down on him before we went to Chicago. He kept a great outlook, but it wasn't looking good. He just wanted to see what they were going to do and move on.

Mick had legal troubles, but that never stopped him from being there for me and whoever needed him.

I'll never forget one night Mick wanted me to bring him some of the money I was holding for him. As I'm on my way to the eastside to meet him, I made a stop. As I walked back to the car, somebody robbed me and took the money and my Yacht-Master gold Rolex.

His care and concern was something I'll never forget, as a few days later he came with not one, but two Rolex watches; one stainless and the other gold. I couldn't believe it! His saying was, "If you ever need money, you'll have something as collateral."

Mick stayed back some, as he had his mother, grandmother, daughters, and grandson to think about. I know Mick cared for me, maybe even loved me. His ways and actions showed that. But I know the case against him was taking a toll on him. In December of 2013, my Big Mick was on his way to federal prison!

I've always told Mick he truly saved my life. Truly not your typical guy who just wanted to get with a woman and buy things for her. But he wanted my future to be secure and free from anything that could keep me away from my children, and I'll always love him for that, as I still talk with him to this day. Never forgetting about him and truly never forgetting the man that invested $8,500 in me to save my life!

God has allowed me to have a few good men in my life, but it always ended up short-lived. I didn't even want to go to Hazel's Place that night. My friend, Big M, said, "Girl, let's go." When I got there, I never wanted the drink Mick sent me, and I surely didn't want to go to the strip club.

I asked God if I hadn't met Mick that night, would you have gotten me the money another way? But we always say, "NEVER QUESTION GOD!"

God uses people to help people, and that's what he placed in my life at that time with Mick. God was covering me from avoiding another prison sentence. And when it was all said and done, Otis Culpeper got them to give me only a year in jail.

Here's where God stepped in again! The Court never wanted to give me work release – in which you can go out in the day and work, pay bills, and even see your family, but being monitored by an ankle bracelet. But, on the day of sentencing, it was a new Judge, and they gave me a year in jail (ten months) with work release, $190 fine, no restitution to the store, and gave me time for my children to get out of school because it was February – allowing me to get affairs in order. "LOOK AT GOD!"

I sat in jail for two days, got called out for work release with an ankle monitor, and started my new job the next day.

After only two months of going out in the day and coming back to jail at night, I received a call that I'm going home on house arrest.

You can't tell me prayers don't change things. It's been a long process, and as of February 2017, I'm finally off probation; now a totally free woman!

I wanted this book to come out around this time because I knew I would be off probation, and I knew that all of my prayers would be answered!

I was supposed to be off probation when I found out I had breast cancer in August of 2014, but for whatever reason, God saw fit for me to be off now. I love you, God. You've been covering me all my life. I didn't know it then like I know now!

Chapter 15
Structure

June 2013

It's 7:30 a.m. at the William Dickerson Detention Facility. The process to let me out for work release took about forty minutes, sometimes shorter. But once they opened that steel door, I was free for twelve hours. Not too free, as I wore a tether (ankle bracelet.)

This was my first morning out after being sentenced to a year in jail (that's ten months), but was granted work release. Two days of sitting and waiting for this part of my sentence to start wasn't so bad.

There's my daughter Tiana, my first born, sitting in my old white Land Rover, waiting on her mama to come out, along with my three boys. I would just look at them every day they picked me up and say, "Thank you, God, that I can at least see them every day, even though I have to go back to the jail at night." I haven't worked a job since I was 16. So, to know people who opened their businesses to me to say I worked there was truly a blessing.

My friend Shon owns a printing and photography studio, so it was easy for me to get in there to say that's where I worked. It was not a "real" job. But, it was somewhere for me to be for eight hours.

See, I had an hour to get dressed, an hour to get to work, and an hour to get back to the jail.

Tiana picked me up and dropped me off every day for about five weeks straight. She would be so tired from going to school, taking care of the boys, and working. She was and still is the epitome of what a daughter should be. Thankfully, her days and evenings didn't last long with picking me up and dropping me off.

July 2013

I got a call from my friend, telling me that Mont's mother passed away. I was hurt for him and wanted to be there for him, but couldn't figure out how I could be there, as I had on an ankle bracelet.

The place where I worked during work-release, Image Masterz, specialized in printing obituaries, and sure enough, my aunt Patty was up there having Shon make Mont's mother's obituary. Now I had an excuse to be there for Mont.

The service was beautiful. Everyone came out to the funeral home in Highland Park. I ran into a few other homeboys, RaRu and Rick.

At this point in time of my life I was hanging with a lot of guys. Never had relationships with any of them. They treated me like their little sister. My "adopted brothers" were Jack, Twan, RaRu, Rick, Lamont, Turf, and Ken.

As everyone is standing around outside the funeral home talking, my friend Micki and I were about to get in her truck and leave, and here came Rick yelling, "Tiff, Tiff, come here!" I said, "What's wrong?" He said, "Nothing, just come here. My friend wants to meet you." I said, "Who?" He's said, "Come on, girl. Come over here."

Rick takes me over to an older, much older gentleman, and said, "Tiffani, this is G; and, G, this is Tiffani." We both said hello at the same time. Rick told G, "She's a good girl, G." "And, Tiff, this is my people. He's good."

I'm thinking in my mind, he's too old. I don't want to talk to him. G and I walked off and talked for a second, and exchanged phone numbers. But I had to let him know, "You might not want to talk to me," as I raised up my long floor-length summer dress above my ankle and said, "I'm on a tether, and I go back to the jail at night, six days a week. I can't come out on Sundays, so you may not want to talk to a chick like me!"

G said, "I don't care about that," in a cool, laid-back tone. I told him, "I'll call you tomorrow afternoon." He said, "I'll probably be sleep, as I work nights. I get off at 7:30 a.m., so call me after you come out."

I told G, "Well, my daughter picks me up from the jail at 7:30, 7:40 every morning. So I'll call you about nine, once I get ready for work." He said, "That's fine." I gave him a hug and said, "Nice to meet you. Talk to you later."

I didn't talk to G the next day as planned, but I did the day after. He wanted to see me, but I didn't want him to come to my apartment where my children were. So I had him come to Lamont's house. I was all over the place, even though I had a tether and was supposed to be at work. I got cocky and started going off, doing my own thing -- hanging with my male friends.

G pulled up to Lamont's house, and I came outside. Lamont had said good things about G, and Rick co-signed along with him, telling me G was a great man. I said, "He's old." They both said at the same time, "That's what you need, stability and structure."

They said, "G has done a lot. He used to be heavy in the streets. He owned the Nile Night Club in downtown Detroit, a restaurant, a host of houses, and more. So that's a man you need to give a chance, and you can stay out of our pockets."

We all laughed, and I told them, "Shut up," as I walked out to G's car. G is a very, very clean-cut man, about five feet, four inches tall; slim build, light-skinned, somewhat balding man, and smells good whenever you see him.

That day was our first time seeing each other since Lamont's mother's funeral and our first date. He asked me could I really be out and not get in trouble? I said, "Yes, I'm okay." He asked was I hungry. I told him, "Yes." So he took me to Joe Muer, a seafood restaurant in downtown Detroit.

The sun was shining as we sat outside the restaurant looking at the water, talking and trying to get to know each other in a few hours before I went back to jail. G told me about his days of owning the Nile Night Club. I told him my friend and I would get dressed with our underage, nineteen-year-old selves and come down to his club, never knowing I would meet him several years later.

I told him about why I had to go back and forth to jail, and how I still struggled with my addiction (the stores.) I said, "I'm working hard to fight off those demons, and I wanted to open a clothing boutique for women, and a host of other things. But I have to get off this ankle bracelet and get off probation to really move forward."

G asked me is it really that hard for me to stop hustling in the stores. I said, "Yes, but I make it my business to try to stay out because it's a trigger for me to walk into a store and see something that I know I can get away with taking."

Then G told me about him being a drug dealer most of his life, and it wasn't until he got shot six times at his restaurant and almost died that he knew he had to get out of the streets. He talked about how he lost his club, houses went into foreclosure, broke up with his woman, having another child late in life, and a host of other things.

After a long hiatus of being off the scene, it allowed him to get himself together. He got a job, worked on his credit, and built himself back up to start life over again with a clean slate. He told me that I could do it too. I sat there in tears as the waiter asked was I okay. I told him, "Yes. I'm crying happy tears." The waiter said, "Good," and walked away.

G said, "Why are you crying?" I told him, "I have family who loves me and wants me to do well, but I have to truly stop hustling and give my life to God, and he'll work it out. You don't even know me, and you're trying to already steer me in the right direction. I'm no fool. I've done stupid things, but I'm no fool. So I appreciate you for these life stories and kind words." He said, "It's nothing. You're still young and have your whole life ahead of you."

I was 36 when I met G, and he was 62. His kind words made me think of my stepfather. Papa was always calm, kind, loving, laid back, and full of wisdom.

I immediately told G, "You remind me of my stepfather, Leo, and I feel like my mother. My mother just wasn't a criminal like me." Our dinner was coming to an end, as I had to get back to the jail.

G told me to call my daughter and tell her she didn't have to take me back to the jail; he would do it, and he would pick me up as well. Tiana said, "Cool." I told G, "Thank you for everything and dinner," and that I would see him tomorrow.

The next day came, and I'm coming out the jail at 7:40. Who was out there? Tiana and G. I don't think Tiana heard me clearly when I said G would come and pick me up. Tiana and the boys said I could go with him. So, they just went back home.

G was so into what I needed and my well-being that I'll never forget it. Every morning he picked me up from the jail and took me to my apartment to get dressed as he sat outside and waited on me.

One day, I stood in my bathroom, needing more money, bills piling up, my children are getting ready to go back to school, and Tiana back to Michigan State.

I yelled to the top of my lungs and said, "Jesus, I need help! I can't afford to take a chance with trying to get money the wrong way! I need a financial miracle, Jesus, right now!" I wiped my tears, took my shower, and went back down to G's car.

He took me to work every day for another month or two -- picking me up from jail, taking me to breakfast, taking me home, and then to work; leaving Tiana free from not driving so much for me. Her job was to take care of the boys, seeing about my autistic son Allen Michael, and my other sons Alexander and Blake.

G did so much for me in a short amount of time. One thing he did after two weeks of dating, he gave me his Capital One credit card and told me, "If I'm not around to give you money, you'll have this." I was too outdone. I needed more, but couldn't ask him. I was about to get put out of my apartment.

I needed to see my Grandma Louise (my mother's mother) more at the nursing home. I moved her up here from Alabama after she had a stroke. I had money from selling her house and everything in it, but the weight on my shoulders was so much until I fell out with family because I wasn't doing my part to be there for my grandmother.

My whole world was falling apart. I took one step forward and got pushed back five. It was too much!

Reality was, I was falling into depression because I wasn't making money.

Trying to still look happy, but in a mess of disaster. I was good at saying and looking like everything is okay, but it wasn't.

My family and I are now okay. We eventually forgave each other. We love each other, and will be there for each other if needed, but it's not the same.

Time is ticking, and I've held off eviction long enough. It's time to go. I had to tell G, and to my surprise, he had a realtor friend who found me another place, and paid for the kids and I to move -- movers and all!

G told me he hadn't been in a relationship with a woman in nine years; no sex, nothing, and this is what he gets when he meets me! We laughed, but here I go again asking a loving and kind man, "Why me?" He said, "Why not you?"

From that day forward, G was and still is a true angel on earth. Now remember, he's older, so he's stuck in his ways. We bump heads all the time. I constantly get on his nerves. But he gave me what I needed, not what I wanted. That's the difference.

By December 2013, G had done so much for us. I didn't have money like I used to, unabling me to get something for someone that's been good to me. So, I started back hustling.

Yes, the dummy writing this book went back into the store getting everything and anything, and money. G saw me bringing stuff in the house and told me after a few weeks, "Are you crazy, Tiffani? You must be. I'm not giving you that much money. What is wrong with you?"

As I looked at all the gifts under the tree, and things spread out all over the living room, I felt bad. But my excuse was, "I'm used to getting my own money, and I have to make that happen. I truly can't depend on a man, G. You have to understand that!" G told me, "No, I don't understand! You talk about God, go to church, pay your tithes, and know God better than me, and this is how you repay God, your children, and me! The ones who are there?

Do you remember your daughter coming to pick you up with your sons? Do you remember? What's wrong with you?! Do you remember how she was tired and stressed at a young age about you?!"

By this time, I am not going back and forth to the jail. I'm on house arrest. So, I'm going in the stores doing dumb stuff.

By the grace of God, having that conversation with G, talking to Tiana, and more so, going to God, giving God my life and saying, "I need you God; come into my life. Take these urges away from me. Make me whole. Change my mind, my thought process. Let me depend on you for everything I need and everything I want. I dedicate my life back to you" … From that day forward, December 23, 2013, I never took anything from another store.

No urges, no triggers. It was all God -- placing my life in His hands. That conversation with G really opened my eyes to want to do better, to want more out of life, and he was willing to ride that wave with me.

G can be stuck in his ways, stubborn, but sweet, kind, and giving -- never a pushover, though. He doesn't go out all the time buying me handbags. Instead, he hands me options on what to do, and how we can make money and build together.

My own look on life is totally different by being with G. And I will say, I've never lived so good and became so at peace, because now I've shed my bad ways, taking my life seriously, and living a more structured life because G brings me stability, something I've never had before.

See, here again, God was looking out for me, keeping me, covering me, and sending someone my way that didn't give me a hard time and trouble; and didn't give me $5,000 here, $10,000 there. God sent stability, peace, and comfort in knowing there was someone for me if I waited on God to give someone to me.

Now, it has not always been perfect between G and I. We almost broke up a few times, but God saw fit for us to be and stay together. He's truly one of the best men that has ever stepped into my life.

Chapter 16
I Wasn't There Then, But I'm There at the End

December 2013

It's 6:00 a.m. I get a hysterical but calm call from my distant friend Lauren (Tiki's daughter). I say "distant friend" because we loved each other, but issues my friend had that I won't disclose tore our friendship apart. Never hating each other, but just not being around for things I never wanted to see her go through.

As I'm listening to Lauren crying, she's telling me, "My mother is unresponsive and she's at Oakwood Hospital in Dearborn." I said, "Unresponsive? What do you mean?"

I went through this with my grandmother when she had a stroke. But my grandmother was awake by the time I arrived in Alabama to see her. I just walked around the house listening to Lauren on the phone. I was trying to get myself together, as I really didn't know what was going on.

I jumped in my truck and flew down to Oakwood Hospital. I get to her room thinking when I turn the corner to walk in I'm going to tease her and say, "What's wrong with you?" That didn't happen.

I turned the corner walking in her room, and there's my friend laying in a hospital bed with tubes coming out of her mouth, eyes closed, and everyone looking sad. I couldn't believe it. I hadn't seen or talked to Tiki in about two years, except for one time in September of 2013 as she called me and told me she loved me and the kids. That was the last time I heard her voice.

Tiki was a light-skinned, beautiful, heavyset woman with a shape. We would always tease her on how you can be this thick with everything of thickness in the right spots, and we'd laugh! She always wore falls (wigs) and virgin hair. She was a beautiful woman who truly didn't need makeup. She was the epitome of a classy, well-dressed woman with a beautiful home and luxury cars. That was our "Tiki doll."

I couldn't believe my friend was laying there, not saying anything. She was truly a woman with a voice and opinion. I came to the hospital every day, talking to Tiki, singing to Tiki, wiping her mouth when saliva would come out, cleaning her face -- constantly talking, asking her to wake up. "Tiki, wake up!"

Tiki had a heart attack and died, but the paramedics brought her back to life after about 20 to 25 minutes. So, no oxygen was getting to her brain. She was brain-dead. The only thing that was keeping her alive were the machines.

Every day I walked in I was expecting her to wake up, but she didn't. The team of doctors spoke to us as a family in a conference room and told us what was best for Tiki.

It's been two and a half weeks that Tiki's been in a coma. What the doctors were saying about her condition was something none of us wanted to hear. Our other friend, Charlotte, was there; another beautiful and strong woman. She was keeping us at ease talking about old times, how Tiki would dress. Just keeping us uplifted, as we all were sad and just wanted to cry all day long. Tiki had a few unwanted old friends there, but we kept the peace. We knew they were only there to be nosy.

S and T, I won't even say their names, as it makes me upset that they were even there. I found out later that S and T were asking for stuff of Tiki's, and she wasn't even dead yet. I would leave the room when they walked in. Even though Tiki and I hadn't talked, we never talked about each other in a bad manner. We just didn't see eye-to-eye. But, I knew S and T were up to no good, there to be nosey.

Week four; it's time to take the tubes out, as Lauren, Tiki's husband Tony, mother Ellen Jackson, son Chol, and brother Shoe-Shoe felt it was time to have Tiki go to hospice. We celebrated Tiki's birthday on December 27, 2013. Our only birthday wish was for her to wake up.

On January 1, 2014, God called Satiki R. Rollins-Jenkins home to glory. Her husband called me and said, "Tiffani, come on down here. Tiki's gone. Hurry up before they take her away." I told Tony I was on my way. I lived 30 minutes away from the hospital, but it felt like I got there in five. I had to see my friend!

I walked in the room and she looked so beautiful with her turban wrap on her head, covered in all white. She was still warm to the touch. As I leaned over to whisper in her ear and kiss her, I told her: "I promise to always have you in my heart. I don't feel guilt of not talking to you for two years because you already knew I've loved you forever, and I promise to be here for your children. Lauren and Chol had a great mother. And with that, I thank you for having me in your life for seventeen years. Love always, your lil' sister, Tiffani."

Tears flowed from my eyes as Lauren asked me to do Tiki's makeup for the funeral, and help her dress her mother. It was an honor, as Tiki and I would always say, "If I die, make sure my eyebrows are right and tight, and make sure I look fly and my hair is done." Never knowing that joke we've said for years would come to pass so soon.

The funeral has come and gone, but my heart still hurts. Lauren and I would talk on the phone, as she was still mourning her mother's death. It was hard on us. As the years have gone by, it's gotten better with her not being here. But we thank God every day for her life, and will always remember the good times and memories of our beloved Tiki doll.

June 2014

I get the call from my cousin Danielle that my grandmother passed away. I had so much going on in my life that I wasn't my grandmother's caregiver anymore. But I received that call to see what I was going to do to bury her.

Nobody stepped up to see about how she was going to be laid to rest. My grandmother had a small insurance policy, but it wasn't enough to lay her to rest properly. It was only $1,000.

When I called, I couldn't even buy flowers with that. So who stepped in? G. He paid for the whole funeral; about $8,000.

My family talked about me so badly when I didn't want to take care of my grandmother anymore. But when it was all said and done, it was me who figured it out financially. Not one dime from my family. Not one. I had no problem taking care of the funeral expenses. I loved her; I just couldn't physically take care of her.

My Grandmother Louise looked beautiful. She was laid out in a mahogany wood casket, a beautiful tan-colored suit, beautiful hair and nails, and lovely flowers. My sister San was there, and barely spoke. I see a lot of family, and we barely spoke. It was all good though. I just wanted the funeral to be over!

I got up to sing. And before I sang, I told my family in front of 200 people, "I love you. No matter what, we're still family. And on this day, she's at rest. No one has to fuss and fight or wonder how things will get done because God's plan worked out!" I was so emotional I couldn't get through the song. My old pastor, Pastor Willis, did the eulogy, and the service was over.

We go across the street to my friend Micki's bar for the repass. I walked up to my sister San, hugged her, and told her in her ear, "I forgive you for everything you did to me growing up."

I don't know if she understood what I was saying, as years earlier she had a nervous breakdown and has mental issues. But it was a relief off my chest. Thank God for change, as I want to truly love everyone. Not wanting to hold grudges because of how people have treated me. I'm not innocent in any of my issues, but I can admit I was wrong, and that's where I am in life now.

See, God allows things to happen to either wake us up, make us realize that tomorrow is not promised, and anything can happen.

Love all the people who have been in and out of your life: family, friends, and folks you don't know, and you'll have a happier and fulfilling life. I truly love everyone with the love of God, no matter what.

Chapter 17
No, Not This

July 13, 2014

I know this is not what I think this is. I'm feeling around and feeling around. I say to myself, "This can't be!" I'm sitting at my dining room table, talking on the phone with my family as we plan to celebrate my sister Lisa's 50th birthday with a party that day. I get off of the phone and tell Tiana to come over. She says, "Ma, what's wrong?" I told her to feel this. She said, "Oh, my God! Ma, what's this?"

A tear came from my eye as I felt a little more. It was a lump in my right breast, and this wasn't the first time I felt this lump. Back in February of 2014, I was in the shower. As I did a self-examination, I felt it then. I called my doctor's office and they scheduled me to come in. Dr. Marshall examined me and didn't feel anything, but told me he would write a script for a mammogram. I said, "great!"

That next week when I was supposed to have the mammogram, I was hanging drapes in my home. I fell off the ladder and tore my ACL (Anterior Cruciate Ligament). Now, at that time I was not thinking about my mammogram. My focus was on my leg, so I ignored the mammogram.

Later that year in May of 2014, I received a call from my friend Sharonda Taylor that her friend Michele McArthur passed away from cancer, and they wanted me to dress her for her funeral. I didn't know Michele, but I was saddened that such a beautiful and successful woman like her had passed away from breast cancer. As I'm dressing

Michele, I whispered in her ear that I was going back to get that mammogram, but I never did.

Going back to July 2014, I'm distraught after finding this lump, but had it in my mind that it wasn't anything. Let's just see what this is. The only people that knew at that time about the lump was Tiana, G, my sister Lisa, and my niece Doni.

A week later I had a mammogram, ultrasound, and then a needle biopsy. I then had the BRCA gene test done. If the BRCA test came back positive, then I would need to have both breasts removed, and my ovaries removed as well. The wait for all these test results seemed like forever. When the results were finally in, my whole world changed!

On August 31, 2014, Dr. Marshall called. He told me I was in my first stage of breast cancer. I was devastated. I called Lisa and Doni and told them to sit down in case they weren't already. I told them I had breast cancer. I cried a little, but Doni cut me off and said, "Tiffani, stop! We serve a mighty God. And as of right now, you're already healed." I told her, "You're right." Lisa was in agreement, but I could tell over the phone she was hurt.

We talked about them being there for me, and that we're going to get through it! We prayed and asked God to step in and put His graceful hands over my life. Heal my body so I can have total victory. We all said "Amen," laughed, and I said, "I got this!"

A few doctor appointments go by, and I'm told that the cancer has spread and it's now Stage 3B, about to approach Stage 4. Now, I know Stage 4 is bad, and Stage 3B is not that much better. I got nervous, and called Doni. And from that point on, she went to every doctor appointment and recorded everything all the doctors said.

Tiana was so hurt. My child had been through so much in her life dealing with me: prison, in and out of jail, my horrible marriage, getting in trouble again, and now breast cancer.

Now, I can take on a lot, but I don't know how Tiana is going to hold up. I think I saw her cry one time, that's it. She really stepped up and became a dependable, responsible, caring and selfless young lady during this now trying time in our life.

All the tests are in, and it's now time for my surgery decision. I was asked if I wanted a lumpectomy (a removal of the tumor), or did I want to remove the whole breast. I immediately told the doctor no to both. I wanted both breasts removed. He asked if I was sure. I told him, "Yes!"

Dr. Sumet was my general surgeon who was going to perform the operation. He made me feel at ease. He told me that his wife had breast cancer, and she opted to have a double mastectomy, so I understand.

I told him my mother had one breast removed, and a few months later got breast cancer in the other breast, and she didn't want to get cut on again. The medications didn't work, and she passed away in 1994. So that's why I'm making my decision to have a double mastectomy.

I met with Dr. Bloom next (my oncologist), and he told me I had to have eight cycles of chemotherapy; one cycle every two weeks.

Then I met with Dr. Trotter (my radiologist). She explained to me that once chemotherapy is over, I'll have a break for a month, and then I'll come to her and have radiation every day, five days a week for ten minutes, for 36 days. I was trying to take it all in, but couldn't. I always had Doni and Tiana there to jot down what the doctors said.

I didn't allow myself to get scared. I just asked God not to let me die. I called my childhood friend, Bianca, and told her. At that time she was still battling breast cancer herself. But she was strong enough to give me advice. The one thing that stood out in that hour-long conversation was she said, "Tiffani, in this battle, you're faced with you cannot be weak-minded. You have to stay strong because the medications and the healing process is going to hit you like a ton of bricks!" I told her, "So it's all mind-over-matter?" She said, "Exactly!"

September 16, 2014

It's surgery day. I've never seen so many doctors and nurses in one room, ever. I can't remember anything the doctors said that stuck in my mind. My whole family was there. They said surgery was about eight hours, including recovery.

I remember my family being there when I woke up. All my friends and family came to see me. The next day after surgery, they truly lifted my spirits with smiles and laughter. The pain medications had me going in and out of sleep. By this time, I'm ready to go home and get some real rest.

Tiana was my "mother" during this whole process. She took care of me, cleaned my scars, cooked for me, took care of the boys, ran my business, did homework with my boys, took them places, and most of all, paid bills with her own money for my household. Tiana truly took over my household because I couldn't do it at that time.

About two weeks have gone by now, and I know I'm going to chemotherapy soon. I called Tiana upstairs and handed her the clippers and told her to cut my hair. She said, "Why, Ma?" I told Tiana that I don't want to see my hair falling out over everywhere, so just cut it. Let's get a head start. As Tiana cut my hair, she started to cry. I told my baby girl, "It's okay. We're going to get through it; I promise."

October 2014

My first day of chemotherapy. I'm looking in my bathroom mirror with nothing on, looking at my scars and saying to myself, "Tiffani, are you ready? It's your first day of chemo."

The whole chemotherapy process was a lot. I had surgery two weeks before to have a port put in my chest, so when I went to chemo treatments, they could administer the medication.

Going to chemo was never pretty. These days would consist of me sitting in a reclining chair and letting the Nurse poke me with an IV type of cord so the chemo meds could be pumped into my body.

The smell of the chemo meds was something that made me want to vomit, but I pushed through. I did this process every two weeks, eight cycles, and after every treatment I had to come back the next day to get my shot of Neulasta, which is used to prevent neutropenia -- a lack of certain white blood cells caused by receiving chemotherapy.

Every time I came home from a chemo treatment, I would be sick. What little bit of hair I had left finally came out. Often times, I would be so paralyzed from the meds, Tiana had to bathe me and clean me up after I went to the bathroom. I truly couldn't walk. I would be so paralyzed and weak.

I would always have a smile on my face, but dying on the inside. I never wanted to give up. I grew tired, but never wanted to give up. I was fine until they tried to cure me.

It's my last day of chemotherapy, January 2015, and we're all excited G was there, finally!

I asked him why he never came to treatments with me. He told me he didn't know how sick I was until he started to see me break down. He said, "I looked at you and you would always be so happy, never really complaining." I told G, "You're my man, and you should have been there! I would have never let you go through something like this by yourself. I understand what you're saying, but I needed you like never before."

See, G, you were here financially, but I needed you physically, emotionally, lifting me up in prayer, holding my hand, and telling me everything was going to be okay."

This was my first time seeing G cry as he told me, "Tiffani, the truth is, I was always going to be around. But I stayed away because I couldn't see you like this." I said, "That doesn't matter. I do understand, but it's life and death, and we need each other."

A month of rest from meds is over. Well, chemotherapy is over. Now it's time for radiation treatments.

February 2015

The break from chemotherapy gave me my strength back. Well some, because I'm still a little weak. I want to feel more independent, so I would drive myself 40 minutes every day, five days a week to lay on the radiation bed 10 minutes, for 37 days. It was a lot!

I'm still having issues with G not being there. We didn't live together at that time, and he gave me excuse after excuse why he wasn't there. I told G I understood how he felt, but I was lying. It grew into arguments. I would tell him that if it was him going through it, and I wasn't here, his family would have hated me and called me everything under the sun. Why I stayed with G after that, I don't know.

After a while, he apologized to me, but on my end it didn't feel sincere. Now, I will say G is a great man and a wonderful provider. But, I tell him all the time, "You have to be a little more compassionate to not just me -- to others as well."

God has a plan for G and I. We still bump heads from time to time, but I know he loves me and I love him. If God puts another adversity in our lives, I just hope G can take it head on; I know I can!

People need to know that your loved ones are a main focus. Be an encouraging factor in one's life! In sickness and pain, heartache and even in gain, you should always support your people, no matter what.

Raising my right arm above my head everyday so I could let the radiation machine burn whatever cancer cells I had left was such a painful process that it gave me third degree burns. Every day, applying Silver Silvadene Cream on my chest to calm the burns. Still, to this day, I can't raise my right arm high.

I'm doing everything at this point to keep staying faithful to God; positive, encouraged, strong, and prayerful. When breast cancer stepped into my life, I never questioned God. I knew this was a great test for a wonderful testimony. Never wanting to give up because it got hard. But, depending on God to hold my hand and see me through.

See, God has never left me in times of trouble, hurt, or pain. Some may wonder, out of all the things I've been through, how can I still love God? Why not love God? It was by God's grace that I'm still here! I'm not broken, "down," losing my mind or ever giving up -- no matter what may come my way!

God gave me a story to tell -- letting the world know of His greatness!

Thank you, God, as I walked out of the Providence Cancer Institute in Novi, Michigan on March 14, 2015. I screamed to the top of my lungs, saying, "Thank you, God, thank you," as Dr. Robert Bloom told me, "Well, Tiffani, everything looks great. You're done, and that means you're cancer-free."

Chapter 18
My Earth Angel

I face-timed Tiana and told her, "Your mama is cancer-free!" I saw the tears flow from her eyes, and all I could do was smile. Tiana didn't say a word as I let her cry. I said, "Baby, it's over." She said, "I know. These are happy tears."

See, Tiana gave up her life for me so many times that I had to ask her, "Do you wish you had a different mother?" Quickly, she said, "No!" This young lady was a mother to my boys when I couldn't be; when I was in and out of jail, prison, and out in the streets. She was always a child who told me she never wanted me to shower and spoil her with material things. She just wanted me at home.

How she stepped in again and became a mother to both the boys and I is something I'll never forget. She's so selfless. She always puts us first. But the ultimate sacrifice she made was leaving Michigan State to take care of me. She went to a community college close to home. She gave everything up for me!

I never told Tiana to do all of these things; It was just in her. No matter what I've done in life, she has always been there. Never disrespectful and always held me at a high standard, even when I didn't deserve it.

See, God, all of your work was not in vain! I stayed faithful to you, even in my wrong. God, I thank you for all of your many blessings, and I thank you truly for the trials. It has made me a strong woman; and with you, I can take on the world and "Bounce Back" from anything.

DEDICATION

I dedicate this book to my beautiful mother, **Dixie Michelle Bell-Wherry,** and to my stepfather, **Leo Wherry**. You both were there for me in times of trouble and happiness. No words can express how much I love and miss you both very much. And for the short time I had you both in my life, I'll always remember the love and kindness you showed me growing up.

Thank you for the foundation you set out in the atmosphere to make me who I am today. Thank you, mom, for stopping me from having an abortion with Tiana. With you doing that, it gave me a pure angle on earth. May your souls rest in peace.

To my best friend, **Satiki Rollins Jenkins**, you gave me the name of my book seven years ago when you told me, "Tiffani, it's not that people don't like you, folks just don't like your 'bounce back.'"

I was only home from prison a few days, not really understanding what you meant, but I know now! I can bounce back from anything. May your beautiful soul rest in peace. Friends for 17 years until death; I dedicate this book to you.

I dedicate this book to my beautiful, smart, successful, strong, loving and caring daughter, **Tiana Michelle Bell**. No words can express the love I have for you. Your dedication to your brothers and I is something I can't explain.

Thank you for all of your love and sacrifice that you've shown me over the years. I truly don't deserve your love, but I'm proud to be your mother, and I pray that all of the work you put in with whatever you do will be blessed right now and for years to come!

I asked you one time, "Do you regret me being your mother?" You quickly said, "No!" I thank you for that and everything else. I'm nothing without you. I love you!

ACKNOWLEDGEMENTS

To my handsome sons, **Allen Michael, Alexander, and Blake**, you make mommy so proud. You make me want to live this life better to watch you grow into wonderful young men. Thank you for keeping me young, happy, and whole. My life would be nothing without you. I love you boys, always and forever!

To **G,** the meanest, sweetest man I know. "THANK YOU" for everything; our home life, how you are there for my children, and love them like you love your own. How you spoil and discipline them, all at the same time. You show the boys how and what a real man is supposed to do and be for his family, and I thank you for that.

No matter what has come our way, we still stand strong as a couple to be able to grow and be strong in this relationship. Thank you again, Ol' Man, as you have now made me the happiest, most stable woman on earth. Thank you for loving me *as I love* you. From the pure pit of my heart, my love forever.

Thank you, to my sister **Nalisa Fuqua**, and my mama/niece, **Doni Brown** (only people who know us understand). Thank you for being there for me since I was 12-years-old, taking care of me before and after my mother passed away. Your undying love is something I'll cherish until the day I die!

I apologize for all of the headaches I gave you and the sleepless nights. You ladies showed me how to be a lady, even when I wanted to be a ghetto fool. You taught me about God when I wanted to go astray. You kept me lifted up in prayer, never judging me nor letting me go.

You both are the true definition of what family is, and we're not "blood." I love you both from the bottom of my heart. Thank you for not letting me go! Love always, your Fannie Rose.

Thank you to my church family, **Second Ebenezer**, and my great leaders, **Bishop Edgar L. Vann** and **Elder Sheila Vann.**

Thank you for your love, kind hearts and leadership. God put me in the right place to grow, enabling me to trust Him like never before!

Made in the USA
Lexington, KY
18 April 2018